Rod

With much love,

Anthony

October 2013

Milly and Me
One Dog and her Man

Milly and Me
One Dog and her Man

Anthony Howard

COUNTRYSIDE BOOKS
NEWBURY BERKSHIRE

COUNTRYSIDE BOOKS
3 Catherine Road
Newbury, Berkshire

To view our complete range of books,
please visit us at
www.countrysidebooks.co.uk

ISBN 978 1 84674 3160

Front cover photograph by Tom Howard

Produced through The Letterworks Ltd., Reading
Typeset by CJWT Solutions, St Helens
Printed by Berforts Information Press, Oxford

THE AUTHOR

ANTHONY HOWARD has worked for fifty-five of his seventy-five years in the theatre, film and television. He has had published a dozen books on the English countryside and the people who live there. Today, with his wife Elisabeth, he is a New Forest small-holder with a flock of Gotland sheep from Sweden, a 1959 Massey Ferguson tractor, a two-acre wood, a few light Sussex hens, a sheep dog called Milly and seventeen acres of sandy meadowland. This is a story about one man, his dog, their adventures and conversations, his memories and their modest achievements. It is dedicated to the finest wife in the world.

AH and Milly out hunting for moles

MILLY AND ME

MILLY is a three-year-old Welsh border collie. She has pretensions to pedigree – though I do not think you will find her in Debrett's or at Crufts. She came to me on our New Forest smallholding from a cramped council house in Andover. Her master there, Luke, loved her just as much as

I do. But, with a night job at a supermarket and two small children, it was impossible for him to give her the care, attention and exercise which she craved. It was heartbreaking for Luke to let her go and he wept salt tears.

When we arrived to collect her on a dark, damp autumn evening, she barked and snarled and curled her lip over her sharp, white teeth. We got her into our car and drove off leaving Luke standing forlorn and miserable by the roadside. Milly sat on the seat looking back at the only home she had known. She was just over a year old.

Now I am seventy-five years old and have never before owned a dog. It is true that I grew up in Suffolk as a farmer's son and that we had farm dogs there. One of them, Bouncer, was my particular favourite and was a much-loved childhood companion. He had his name because, searching for rabbits in the growing crops of wheat and barley, he used to leap upwards on four legs and would appear above the corn like a jack-in-a-box.

Milly arrived nervously at her new home at the top of Hampshire's New Forest. Highly strung is an overused description but it suits her perfectly. And she is mischievous as well. She is a barking dog and, for me, living where I do in some isolation, that is no bad thing. But not everyone agrees. My wife, Elisabeth, is one of those. She carries from childhood the nickname of Willy – her younger sister could not manage to say 'Elisabeth'. Soon after the collie joined our family I said to her in a loud, firm voice, 'Milly, come here at once.' Willy emerged down the stairs. 'Don't you dare talk to me like that,' she said. Since then the two nicknames have caused regular difficulties.

Milly settled in well. She is a beautiful creature with a classic, white island round her black nose and stretching up between her eyes to her forehead. She has the sharp challenging gaze of a wolf. At dusk it looks as though there is a candle burning behind her eyes as they reflect the setting sun. She is both territorial and protective. I believe that she would die for me, as I know I would for her. We live up a track which leads nowhere off a No Through Road with views of the forest at every point of the compass. So there is no passing traffic – just the daily visit of Chris, the postman, the odd delivery van and a few visitors.

Milly likes to make her presence felt whenever anyone comes. She runs

Autumn meadows at Drove Cottage

like an antelope beside our bumpy drive barking furiously. Once somebody has come through the gate and she has nipped the toe of their boot a couple of times, she settles down and is happy again until the next arrival sets her off.

Like most border collies Milly is a glutton for exercise. She runs elegantly and smoothly with very little up and down movement over the ground. She cannot lie down, even in the warm sunshine, for more than a few minutes. Then she is off and on the move again. Nobody is allowed to be doing anything in our house, in our half-acre of garden, in our five meadows or in the two-acre wood without her knowing what is happening and why. To say that she is inquisitive would be a gross understatement. And she has a spooky ability to know what is going on. When I leave the house to take food or water to our handsome, black and white Light Sussex chickens, she senses immediately what I am doing and is out and guarding the hen run well before I get there. If I am fetching hay for the sheep, bringing in logs for the fire, heading out to break ice on the water troughs or taking a letter to the post box, she will always know and will act and behave accordingly. Intelligent may be the wrong word for her. Intuitive might be more accurate. But she is certainly unusually bright and clever. And I would guess that she has a vocabulary of some thirty words. I am not claiming that she can talk – although, with her eyes, ears and tail, she can do the next best thing. But I am saying that she can understand a large number of words and conversations. There is a famous sheepdog story from the Lake District in the 1930s. Bad weather with snow was forecast. The farmers and their dogs went out with some urgency to bring in their flocks from the hills. They worked all morning and stopped briefly for a bite of lunch at noon. On the way into the barn with their sandwiches one man told his friend that, first thing after their break, they should go up to High Peak to bring the sheep down from that exposed hillside. Afterwards, setting out from the yard, they found that the oldest and wisest of their dogs was missing. They went round the back and there he was guarding the whole of the High Peak flock. He had heard those two words, drawn his own conclusions and had headed out on his own to bring the animals in while his master ate his meal. I like to believe that Milly is as intelligent as that wise, old dog. She certainly

Cover of 'Country Ways in Hampshire and Dorset'

understands a very great deal of what I say and, strange to tell, of what I think as well.

Milly knows when I am angry and she alters her behaviour accordingly. Because I have been taught to try to hide my annoyance, human beings, in the main, do not know that I am cross. The dog, on the other hand, makes herself scarce until the storm has passed. A week or two back a visiting fox or badger took one of my beloved Light Sussex hens while we were away from home for a couple of hours. I was as angry as a man can be who has lost a chicken to a fox, and I vowed that I would shoot him with my rifle or my 12-bore from the spare room window next time he came by. Usually, with an event of that kind, Milly would be rushing self-importantly around and demanding to be kept informed and to be at the centre of things. But, because she knew that I was so irritated, she vanished. And she did not reappear until what remained of the chicken had been safely buried in the compost heap. When she did rejoin our little world she was uncharacteristically quiet and well-behaved, as though she was trying to soothe me and to make amends for this small domestic tragedy. When it comes down to the basics of human life, dogs are often a great deal more sensitive than people.

I get up between 6.15 and 7.30 in the morning, depending on what the day ahead holds. Monday is housework. Tuesday helping out at the local junior school. Wednesday is devoted to tidying our local churchyard, where our granddaughter, Maisy, lies buried. Thursday brings tennis. Friday is sometimes shopping day, sometimes gardening and, occasionally, more tennis. And the weekends are the weekends with church bell ringing on Sunday morning. I shave downstairs in the laundry-hung bathroom beside the kitchen. This is also Milly's bedroom. She sleeps on a cosy eiderdown beside the bath. When I come down I receive a royal welcome from her. But then I have to scrape my face with the back door wide open whatever the weather, so that she can have the run of the garden and the downstairs rooms. Every now and again she trots in, stands on her hind legs as I peer sleepily into the mirror and gives me a warm hug with her front paws. It is very endearing and a perfect way to start the day, even if it is a little cold in the depths of winter with the wind and rain blowing in through the kitchen door.

Milly is mad about our small flock of sheep – but more of that later. She is also keen on the chickens, though they are not so easy to round up as the sheep. And she clearly believes that human beings need sorting out and organising in whichever direction she decides that they ought to be going. In the absence of anything living, she has to be content with a ball. I used to be a keen cricket and rugby player. Both games are beyond my reach in my old age, so now I play tennis instead. I manage two or three sessions a week and thoroughly enjoy a sport which I used to consider a bit soft – even though I can proudly boast that my dear, old mother won the ladies' doubles at Wimbledon in 1932. In addition to wielding a racquet, I still have a pretty good throwing arm from cricketing days and there are, of course, plenty of

When she plays cricket, Milly likes to field at cover point

old tennis balls around our house. Any time of the day or night Milly will chase and retrieve and often chew to death these well-used missiles. She is tireless. I am not. I go on throwing for her until my shoulder muscles, my mind and my patience are all exhausted. And still she wants more. Sometimes she will bring a ball back to be thrown again. At other times, out of mischief, she will hold onto it and will goad me into chasing her round and round our garden. She may or may not know that old blokes need exercise. But she certainly makes sure that I get mine. She has the stamina of the Sphinx. I, alas, do not. So Milly always wins. I fear that it may be bad for her character. She is certainly very conceited about it. And I sometimes imagine that I can see her thinking, 'Well, he is not up to much. If he does not watch out, I shall be looking for someone younger and fitter to play with.'

After dark, when I am reading or writing or listening to the radio or to music or watching television, Milly often asks to go out. Usually it is because she is bored. Like her master, she has a low boredom threshold. When I get up from my comfortable armchair in front of the log fire and open the kitchen door for her, she stands there waiting for me to go first. But I do not want to go out into the cold night. Milly does not care about the dark. She wants to go walking or hunting for moles or, at the very least, rushing round the garden with me in lukewarm pursuit. I am not prepared to do any of these energetic things. So Milly, with a dog's equivalent of a shrug of the shoulders, turns and comes back into the house, which, by then, has received an unwelcome blast of freezing air. Sometimes, it is true, she will go out on her own at night to have a look around and to see if there are any unwelcome deer, badgers or foxes in our meadows. After a few minutes and just when I have settled back into my armchair, there will be a scratching on the French window and her little face will be peering in at me and telling me, I swear: 'Can't you see that it's cold out here? There you are sitting in the warm while I am out here chilled to the bone. For goodness sake hurry up and let me back in.' This performance can happen four or five times in an evening. And on Tuesdays, when I bicycle home from the local school, the same small head, with a couple of 'woofs', pokes through a gap in our blue, cast-iron gate, examines me closely to see whether I might have been doing something in which she would like to have been involved, and asks gruffly: 'Where on earth have you been? Here am I wanting to get on with things and you just disappear down the drive on that ridiculous bicycle. For goodness sake can't you learn to be your age?'

One of the things I have tried to learn in life is to listen. And I have always been pleased with the words that Jung is supposed to have said to Freud: 'Up until the age of forty-five or fifty I always worried what other people thought about me. Now I have realised that it is far more important what I think about other people.' So many folk are unjustifiably pleased with themselves and with the sound of their own tedious voices. Milly did not used to be a listening dog. She was, in her own eyes, an all action, centre-of-attention heroine. And she was quite pleased with herself as well. That remains. Everybody was keen to advise us about how to train her. Some of the tips were useful. Some were nonsense. All were stupidly expensive. Without exception everyone insisted that dog 'treats' were an essential part of any training. I entirely disagree. In the case of dogs, kind words and cruel ones butter lots of parsnips. And, living in a land where the pavements of the towns are cluttered with human hippopotamuses, we do not also need more than our share of gross and overweight dogs. In any case Milly responds far more to love and encouragement – and sometimes to trenchant criticism – than she does to bribery. Over time she has learnt to listen and to work out whether she is dealing with the good guys or the bad guys. People sometimes think that dogs work more with their eyes than with their ears. Again I disagree. Milly's eyesight is sharp and accurate. Her hearing is uncanny. Because she is relatively low on the ground she cannot always see what is going on. But she can work out with her ears what is happening and she reacts accordingly. It is not a quick process but, over time and with much patience and many encouraging words, as well as a few harsh ones, she has learnt and is still learning obedience, discipline and self restraint. This is an infinitely more effective method of training than the lazy way of endless feeding of revolting titbits. It is better for the health of the dog and for the physical and mental well-being of the master.

I have spent six of the last ten years afflicted with clinical depression.

With the help and affection of my wonderful family and friends, of loving doctors and psycho-therapists and with the intake of truck loads of heavy-duty pills, I am now in the clear and am no longer swallowing any medicine at all. I am one of the lucky ones and keep my fingers crossed about the future. It is wonderful to be free of this monster disease, which I would not wish on my most hated enemies – even on Bush, Blair, Campbell, Rumsfeldt, Cheyney, Hoon, Rove, Brown or Straw and the other Iraq maniacs. (I would however wish them all a speedy visit to the International Criminal Court at the Hague and a long sojourn behind bars.) And dear Milly has played her important part in my recovery and in helping me to remain as sane as ever I am. Elisabeth, my wife of half a century, firmly believes that, but for the collie, which she sometimes finds quite tiresome, I would have had a relapse by now. Who is to say whether she is right or wrong? All I can observe and experience is the joy in my heart when I find Milly waiting patiently for me at the five-bar gate into our meadows where I have left her while I take a bale of hay to the sheep. As I leave her I say, 'Stay here Milly.' And there she stays. I may be gone fifteen or twenty minutes but, when I return, there she is, bright-eyed, loyal and loving. I cannot find the words to describe how much that extraordinary friendship means to me. I have felt the benefit of it in my heart and in my mind. It is the most healing of relationships. A similar experience happens when we are playing on the lawn with the tennis balls. Sometimes Milly will chase the ball back and forth, back and forth until exhaustion sets in. But now and again she will tease me by holding onto the ball with her teeth and refusing to let me chuck it across the grass for her. The mischievous, playful and amused look in her eyes as she plays this game is like the demeanour of a much-loved and high-maintenance child. The soothing influence of this behaviour on my mind is a constant wonder and surprise to me. I do not understand it. All I can say for sure is that it is a reality and that it has an amazing, healing effect on me. I am lucky indeed to have such a good friend. And, in the evening, when the day is over and I am sitting with my book in front of the fire where our home-split beech and birch logs are burning brightly, sometimes, if she is feeling generous and sociable, she clambers up onto our battered, fifty-year-old sofa, lays her head on my lap and – that rare thing for her – relaxes. Greater happiness than that can no man fairly expect.

THERE are a good number of people in this wicked world – most of them rich – who have a financial interest in doing their jobs as slowly as they possibly can. Bankers, solicitors, accountants, lawyers and several more professions all charge heavily by the hour. The more time that they can convince their customers that they have taken to do a job, the more money they can charge them. These are creatures who expect to be paid plenty of pounds by the minute. Why we continue to allow them to get away with it I shall never know? It is a mystery. Milly, I am proud to say, is not like that at all. Nor, I hope, am I. With her, speed is of the essence. She likes eating and drinking but she gobbles her food and slurps her water. She loves to find out what is going on. But she never walks. She always runs. She hears a noise which she does not recognise, and, then and there, she must discover what it means. This instinct has many advantages. If the hens cackle, as they do, because a fox or a badger is nearby, Milly will be on the case in a flash. If she is in the house and the door is closed, she will scream to be let out so that she can go and confront the intruder. If I leave her at home asleep – an infrequent occurrence – and go out to the shed in the meadow to start up the red 1959 Massey Ferguson tractor, the engine only has to turn over once and she is at the fence demanding to come along for the ride. The truth is that she is insatiable. No experience, however small and dull, is boring for her. It may be the enthusiasm of youth. But it is hugely more attractive than the languor and the seen-it-all, done-it-all attitude of most modern teenagers with their violent computer games and irritable mobile phones and text messages. Milly is better company than a football team of them – a game played by morons for the entertainment of cretins.

Above all, perhaps, she is a clever dog – not in the intellectual sense of course but in the street-wise, instinctive meaning of the word. People who are born clever or who learn wisdom through their education are often dull and boring. No great harm in that, though listening to them banging on about their pet subjects makes me lose the will to live. Out of duty I am a school governor and our meetings are about as exciting as a pudding which we

Milly enjoys helping with the Spring cultivations

called 'dead baby' at the place where I was educated. Milly, on the other hand, is always thrilling company. She is never predictable or dreary, though she can be aggravating and annoying at times. It is a curiosity to me that you seldom, if ever, come across a boring animal whereas you count yourself lucky to meet human beings who are not a living cure to insomnia. I think that this is because, in the main, creatures are not self-centred, whereas men, women and children for the most part are interested in themselves, their comforts, their material wellbeing, their greed and their self-indulgence. Milly is a curiously unselfish dog. Yes, she becomes jealous if I show undue affection towards a visitor of any kind and certainly she is quite keen on her food. But she does not demand to be the centre of attention as so many people do, and she is willing to serve and to work without asking for any reward. The words, 'Good girl Milly – I am proud of you,' are all she needs to experience happiness after a long winter's day in the cold and wet. I have seen her drag herself in from the meadows on a filthy December evening, her coat heavy with icy rain, her paws caked with mud and her head weary with well-doing and immediately give tail-wagging affection and fond love to me and my friends and family. There are not many people on whom I can rely to behave like that.

First and foremost, of course, Milly is a sheepdog with all the mystical instincts, which that description and name imply. As far as I know, she had never seen a ewe, a ram or a lamb before she came to our patch. But today, as soon as she trots into a meadow where our small flock is grazing, her pointed chin sinks down onto her front paws as she crouches, and her eyes seem to change shape and size and intensity. They become what I imagine a killer shark's eyes would look like as it circles its prey in the Pacific Ocean. All my life I have heard tell of the magical properties which collies possess and I have watched with fascination as shepherds bring in vast flocks from the hills with a couple of dogs. Now was the chance to discover if I could do it myself – or at least supervise something along those lines.

I found a sheepdog trainer called Robert Putnam at Kirdford near Petworth in Sussex. He lived in modest discomfort inside a battered caravan surrounded by bailer twine, brambles and barbed wire. He was of the earth earthy (as my father used to say) and reminded me of my childhood hero, Tommy Beeton, who was the tractor driver on my father's Suffolk farm. We named our son, Tom, after him. Stocky, crinkly-haired and walnut-skinned, Tommy could neither read nor write. But he was the wisest and kindest man that I have ever met. He taught me to shoot and to fish, to drive a tractor, to work with ferrets, to read the weather and to be polite. I owe him an enormous debt of gratitude. He was a genuine, country gentleman and I loved him.

Robert Putnam examined Milly with care. She returned the compliment, baring her teeth. He asked her age and I told him that she had recently had her first birthday. He nodded and sent off one of his frighteningly obedient dogs to fetch a bunch of a dozen crossbred ewes from the far side of his

Suffolk tractor driver Tom Beeton and his family

waterlogged meadow. They trotted over to us looking a trifle bored as though this was an everyday routine for them, which, I discovered over the next few weeks and months, indeed it was. While Milly and I watched, he ordered his dog to round the sheep up to the left with a softly spoken 'Come by' and then to the right with an equally gentle 'Away'. In between, he ordered the collie to 'Lie down' and she immediately flattened herself to the ground, remaining there motionless. Then he came over and tied a light, fifteen foot cord to Milly's collar, went over and stood with his sheep, looked Milly straight in the eye and said 'Away'. She hesitated for a moment in her crouched position and then leapt up and circled the sheep to the right. I could scarcely believe what I was seeing. Then he made her lie down and next time do the round-up to the left with 'Come by'. If she went wrong – and she did from time to time – he trod on the cord with his heavy boot and brought her up short with a jerk to the neck. The sheep had clearly been through this a thousand times before and they, with their skills, played an important part in the training. Soon Robert involved me in the teaching, telling me with some force that the dog owners were always harder work for him than their dogs. And it soon became quite clear that Milly was far cleverer than I was at this intricate dance. Quite simply it came naturally to her.

Over the next dozen or so weeks we drove the long journey to Sussex – Milly and me – and, slowly in my case and swiftly in hers, made the transition from learners to adequate to not-too-bad. And that is how we stand today. It is a moving sight, which brings tears to my eyes, to position myself in the far corner of one of our meadows and send Milly off to bring our flock of sheep over to me. I can say with confidence that this is the highlight of her life. She dashes away circling to the left or the right, depending on which way I have asked her to go. Soon, over the hill, I see a row of small heads bobbing up and down as the sheep come running towards me. Behind them Milly weaves backwards and forwards, to the left and to the right, keeping them together and nipping their heels if they show any signs of resistance. Soon they surround me and Milly circles them and then, when I ask her, lies down on guard and on full alert for any disobedient behaviour. I always feel as though I have just conquered Everest although, in truth, I have done nothing except to stand waiting in the corner of the field. I have never experienced any sensation like watching my own much-loved sheepdog doing the job which she clearly adores.

Every day, some time between six and seven o'clock, depending on what is happening later, Milly and I set out on our morning round. Before we leave the house she feels the need constantly to interrupt my shaving by jumping up with her front paws on my waist just to make sure that she is still loved. Then we go together to feed our Light Sussex hens, which are grumbling softly for their breakfast of wheat, barley and maize. They are beautiful birds with white feathers, redder than red combs and black collars and tail feathers. Waking up to their early muttering is as comforting as listening to the breaking of the waves on the sea shore when we are on holiday in my mother's homeland, Greece. The eggs which they lay make it certain that we shall never again buy and eat the ersatz ones provided by the supermarket. The sad side of keeping chickens comes when, at the age of three years or thereabouts, they have reached the end of their useful lives and they are slaughtered. It is not a task which I enjoy, but it is the fate of most animals which you see in farmers' fields as you pass by, and the meat which they provide as old boilers is excellent if it is sensibly cooked. Next, on our early circuit, are the sheep. The most we have had is thirty. As I write we are the proud owners of just seventeen, which means that we have one animal for each of our precious acres. In our part of the New Forest with its sandy soil it is important to understock the land. There are places nearby, which, by the end of the winter, look as though the All Blacks have been playing an international rugger match against the Springboks. This is farming at its worst. Our sheep are from Gotland, an island off the west coast of Sweden.

Unlike the Welsh Speckled-faced Beulahs, which we bred before and which were as wild as stags, these are quiet, gentle and inquisitive animals. They have black faces, some of them with a white star on their foreheads, and silver fleeces which are prized by knitters everywhere.

Milly and I have to count them, to make sure that none of them are lame and that they have not pushed their way under the electric fence into the wood where the rhododendron leaves are lethal to their health, and to check on their hay and their salt and mineral licks. They are friendly beasts and come crowding round as we do our duties. If they become too friendly, Milly is inclined to nip their small hooves and ankles. One advantage these sheep have, now that we are old, is that they are lighter and therefore easier to handle than other breeds. When we are clipping their feet or dosing them or shearing or trimming the wool around their bottoms, they are far easier to handle than Beulahs or Suffolks or any of the other sheep that we have been lucky enough to own over forty or so years.

There are some two miles of fences round our meadows and wood and guarding the small stream in the valley. So next, Milly and I have to walk along them to make sure that they are secure and standing firm. We often have deer in our fields – up to a dozen fallow and roe – and sometimes a pure white fallow, which looks like a ghost early on a dark winter's morning.

Speckled faced Beulah sheep

Sometimes we spook them and they charge away, hurdling the wire and occasionally breaking fence posts or flattening the stock fencing. All this has to be noticed and noted so that, when daylight comes, I can come out with the tractor and trailer to make the necessary repairs. If the winter gales have brought down a tree or a mighty branch in the wood I shall need to return later with the chain-saw to cut it into logs for our open fires, which provide us with more than fifty per cent of our heating.

Once Milly and I were out with a visiting hound – an Arabian saluki,

Gotland sheep with their mistress

trained to hunt gazelle across the sands of the Sahara. He is a gentle creature and the colour of golden treacle. He has the size and look of a greyhound, but is less ugly. His name is Prince. We were walking through our neighbour's pine wood when a small herd of deer trotted across the ride ahead of us. Prince and Milly both crouched, fingers on the trigger, and then they were away. Milly is fast – very swift indeed. But Prince had twice the speed. The deer were crashing through the brambles and the undergrowth. Prince was close to the shoulder of the tail-ender when I last saw them dashing through the trees. I always carry a whistle on a string around my neck. So I blew and blew again. A quarter of an hour later a guilty, filthy and exhausted Milly trotted back through the puddles. She was not as apologetic as she should have been. But there was no sign of Prince. This was not his territory so, unlike Milly, he would not know his way home. And, in the excitement of the chase, he could easily be lost. I waited for half an hour, shouting and whistling, and then headed for home. Elisabeth and I alerted the neighbourhood – friends and villagers. Nothing. We waited. A few hours later the phone rang. There had been a possible sighting at suitably named Stagbury Hill, a couple of miles away across the forest. We walked there as fast as our legs would take us. Still no sign of Prince. We were close to despair. How were we going to tell our daughter, whose dog he was? The day dragged by. Fourteen hours later, at ten o'clock that night, there was a call from a lady in a house on Canada Common five miles away and close to the pub, the Rockingham Arms. There was a large, gold-coloured dog lying immobile in her driveway. We drove over and, to our joy, retrieved a very tired deer hound. He had to be lifted with some difficulty into the back of our car.

I have arthritis in my left knee. There is no cartilage left between one knobbly bone and the other. Seventy-five years of wear and tear, of rugger and cricket, of work and play, have done their worst. I limp. On our morning rounds, Milly, who is a great imitator, has begun to copy me. She drags her hind leg because, I suppose, she believes that, since her master can do no wrong, this is the way to walk. At first I thought that she must have picked up a thorn or a splinter. I could find nothing. I took her to our charming Mid-Forest vet. Milly is tetchy about being examined. But no damage could be found. I gave her anti-inflammatory pills on the vet's instructions and at great expense. Still she limped. Then, one morning, I made a huge effort to walk without lurching to the left. Within ten minutes she was as right as rain. I have experimented several times between limping and walking truly. It always seems to work. So the only conclusion I can draw is that she is copying me.

Here is another example of this quality in my dog. We have a mole problem on our sandy land, which is simple to burrow through. I like moles. They are endearing creatures. But their mole hills ruin our pasture land and, when we start to make hay in the summer, their earth gets into the bales, making the dried grass unpalatable to sheep and cattle during the winter months. I often wish that I could take the little creatures aside and explain the problem to them. But of course I cannot. So I trap them. Over the years and slightly to my shame I have killed hundreds. It is not a difficult skill but, if you are to have success, you must get it right. You need to find the runs with a pointed stick between the piles of earth pushed up by the tunnelers. It is no good trapping in the molehills themselves. Once you have found the narrow passage you need to dig down to it and put the trap into the hole before covering it up again and marking it carefully with a stick. When Milly first saw me doing this job she watched with fascination. The second time she tried to help me dig the hole. Now there is no stopping her and, whenever we have a new invasion in our meadows, she is at it with a will pulling at the turf with her paws and her teeth. So far, however, she shows no sign of being as successful as I am – more is the pity.

On our early morning journey, when we reach our half way point, there is a rusty, metal gate – often our turning-for-home goal. Sometimes, if there is time, we go over the stile beside the gate and walk for another mile. If we are going to head home I always touch the steel post. Milly sees this and immediately turns back. If I do not put my hand on the gatepost she clambers through the stile and on we go. Another helpful skill that she has developed is in helping me to gather giant fir cones. They are used for decorations at Christmas by the children at our daughter's infant school in Wandsworth in south-west London. Milly is clever enough to have realised that normal cones are not needed. Only the big, chunky ones will do. Often, when I have been disappointed and have failed to find one of these prizes, she will come trotting along with one firmly clamped between her teeth and will hand it to me. Then, when I have been sure to tell her how clever she is and how proud of her I am, she will scamper away and return with a second one. She never goes back for a third because she knows that there is no room for three in the narrow pockets of my khaki dungarees.

I HAVE read stories about vicious, cruel and greedy dogs. Indeed, I know that people have been killed and fearfully injured in attacks by them. My observation is that these are rare events and that most dogs, if treated properly, are well behaved and civilised. It is true that Milly is territorial and barks and bares her teeth at strangers. It is a fact that she will sometimes lie inside the open kitchen door and will nip at the feet of visitors as they come and go. I am working hard to cure her of this irritating and anti-social vice. I wish that I could offer such minor criticisms of human beings – of politicians and their spiteful propagandists, who take our beautiful country and its mainly brave soldiers into vicious overseas wars, in which tens of thousands of innocent civilians perish, on the basis of bare-faced lies and deception. Of bankers, lawyers and accountants, all with their snouts deep in the trough, who charge a couple of hundred pounds an hour for their time and who, for that reason, make sure that every job that they undertake lasts as many expensive weeks and months as possible. Can it really be the case that while, on the international stage, the United Kingdom declares its abhorrence of torture, we, together with the Americans, are too cowardly to commit our own atrocities and send our victims to distant lands to be mistreated there in a foul act, which is laughingly called 'extraordinary rendition'? Our country has recently expressed its regrets to the men of the Mau Mau in Kenya for the torture and death which we visited on them in the middle of the last century. We have paid the survivors, all in their eighties and more today, a paltry twenty million pounds in compensation. And yet we continue to have our opponents flown to far off lands to be grossly maltreated and we carry on murdering without trial from the safety of unmanned drones our perceived enemies. Sometimes these turn out to have been Afghan wedding parties. And we dare to protest that we are the world's civilised nations. I do not believe that any dog, given that it had the facility, would behave in such a way. I can remember, on his first day in office, the American president saying that the prison of injustice on Cuba, Guantanamo Bay, where over a hundred and fifty men – innocent until they are proved to be guilty – have been held without trial for more than five years, would be shut down within a year. Those of us who had marched against the confidence trick wars in Iraq and Afghanistan cheered. Today the concentration camp continues to do its dirty work. America rightly mourns and wears sackcloth when its school children are mown down in the regular mad massacres by its own citizens proudly bearing arms. But there is scarcely a murmur when some skilled airman in Nevada mistakenly zaps a bunch of Afghan civilians, slaughtering dozens of innocent men, women and children. I wonder how long it will be before one of these long distance drone 'heroes' is decorated for gallantry in the face of the enemy. And I puzzle over how many of our leaders – men apparently without consciences – make use of the balm of the confessional to allow them to sleep easy at night. Milly and other dogs rest gently during the dark hours and deserve their peace. I hope that those blood-stained 'statesmen' and their sycophantic advisers do not. They deserve everything which I hope is coming to them – with any luck at the International Criminal Court.

Human beings in positions of power are usually – though not always – arrogant creatures. Dogs are certainly tail-waggingly pleased with themselves when they are praised. But they are not conceited and vain like men – and sometimes women – in authority are. The vanity of dogs, if it exists, is harmless. The pride and self-adoration of people leads to Vietnam, Iraq, Afghanistan and the collapse of great banks and businesses. It is a deeply unattractive and dangerous vice. It is something which should be dealt with in the kindergarten, but too often permeates the White House and 10 Downing Street.

I spent nearly fifty years of my life writing and directing films and TV programmes. I worked on something approaching three thousand hours of material in various guises. I was also fortunate enough to have a dozen books published. I worked with hundreds of different men and women. Scores of them were what today we would insult by calling celebrities. To take just a few at random – Archbishop Makarios of Cyprus, George Best, the Beatles, Fiona Fullerton, Bill Oddy, Prime Minister Jim Callaghan, Shirley Williams and Robert Maxwell. The talented folk in my industry specialised. As you can tell from that list, I did not. I was what in football – that game of ping pong for adults – they call a utility player. But I had a wonderfully amusing working life, which never felt like hard labour. Of all the famous people whom I came to know – some of them well, others briefly – a few were charming, none that I can remember were sincerely modest and many were truly foul, unappetising and overwhelmingly pleased with themselves.

Once upon a time I was working with a veteran BBC and ITV reporter on a one-hour documentary for Channel Four. The subject was an old and splendid Sussex countryman, a magnificent gun shot, a prodigious gardener and a man with more skills and talents than any half-dozen Oxford and Cambridge graduates. Our story was about badgers and foxes, springtime and harvest, hunting and fishing, cart-horses and village weddings. It was a rural idyll. We filmed throughout a long year in all weathers and seasons. The minutes were filled with superbly captured images by the cameraman of the English countryside in all its summer moods and winter wildness. When my journalist colleague saw the finished product all he did was to complain that his face had not appeared once in the film. And he certainly was not a Tom Cruise look-alike. In spite of this grave omission, I am glad to report that the programme was well received.

In the 1980s, I was made responsible over the course of a year for three hours of live children's television every Saturday morning. This may not sound much of a challenge and, thirty years on, who gives a damn? But it was, in fact, a huge undertaking. We were a team of forty plus and we worked flat out. That was the year when I had one day off in the whole twelve months – a Sunday if I remember correctly. And, on New Year's Eve, my beloved boss, Jeremy Wallington (famous at Granada Television for running *World In Action*), came into my office, handed me a brown envelope and said, 'Thank you for a fine spell of work.' Inside was the wherewithal for a holiday for my wife and me to travel anywhere in the world that we wished to go, together with £1,000 spending money – an even greater sum then than it is now. We set off in April for much-loved Cyprus, and had a wondrous fortnight there. On the Saturday show we had to have a team of presenters. No one person can keep an audience, mainly made up of children, happy for a long 180 minutes. One of these so-called professionals used to rejoice in the habit of summoning me down to the studio floor during a commercial break – and remember this was live entertainment – and threatening not to take up the show again when we came back on the air in two or three minutes. He believed that he had power because of the situation we were in and he loved to use it to get his own way or to obtain special favours. That is the hallmark of the bully across the centuries. Needless to say, he was not allowed to get away with it. He was a nasty piece of work.

No dog would behave in such a way – certainly not Milly. All she pines for is a pat and a word of encouragement. When it comes to a choice for me between the self-proclaimed high and mighty and a Welsh border collie, there is no competition – none at all. And that goes for the so-called great and good as well.

A Winchester friend wrote asking me whether I thought that wives or dogs were better companions for men. I replied that, of course, dogs are better company. They are wiser, less argumentative, more interesting, funnier, more helpful and usually better looking. They are also happy for you to eat lunch in your filthy, working clothes, and less demanding in bed. I know that there could be a similar litany written by women about the choice between men and, say, cats. But, I told my friend that there were two outstanding exceptions to my rule – his wife and mine, Sarah and Elisabeth. I also wondered if he would give me an 'A' star mark for my reply.

Elisabeth undoubtedly has a favourite sheep – probably more than one – which she prefers to me. And who can blame her? He is stocky for a Gotland, with the blackest of black faces and a shining, white star above his eyes. He is a handsome fellow and I hope that one day she might take him to the New Forest Show at Brockenhurst. I am sure he would earn a winner's rosette. Gotland sheep are browsers – rather like goats – though far more agreeable and better behaved. They are happy enough munching grass and hay – even far gone winter's pastures in January and February. They will commit crimes for a trough full of sugar beet pulp. But what they most enjoy is easy access to ivy or a beech hedge or laurel or rhododendron. And

Pedro, Elizabeth's favourite lamb

therein lies the problem. The beautiful shrub from the Greek island of Rhodes grows happily in our sandy, acid-laden forest soil. When our new sheep first arrived a couple of years ago we turned them out onto the lush grass in our best meadow, which adjoins the small wood. They nosed around cheerfully enough for a few minutes and then headed straight for the trees. Within seconds they had begun to devour the thick, green leaves of our massive rhododendrons. Luckily Elisabeth, by some precious female instinct, recognised the danger. With great difficulty we separated the animals from the bushes, many of which are twenty feet high. So there is no shortage of poisonous grub. The next day we had some very sick sheep. So bad was it that we thought for a while that we were going to lose a couple of them. In the end, because they are fit and healthy beasts, they survived. But it is for this reason that, when Elisabeth takes her favourite, Pedro, out of the meadow, she always has him on a halter and lead. She can direct him to the ivy and beech but keep him away from the bad stuff. Milly is seriously puzzled by these garden excursions. She is well used to and quite accomplished at dealing with a bunch of sheep. She is not sure what to make of Pedro on the end of a rope. So she circles him and my wife slowly and warily taking the odd nip at his hooves and looking appalled when she gets soundly scolded for doing what she imagines to be her duty. It is like a comedy act on one of the few, less embarrassing, Radio 4 'funny' programmes at 6.30 in the evening. As a matter of fact, that sets too low a standard. It is a great deal more amusing than that.

Along with Ernest Hemingway, George Orwell is one of my literary heroes. They are both masters of English prose and they sweated blood to achieve their memorable masterpieces. George Orwell wrote: 'A normal human being does not want the kingdom of heaven; he wants life on earth to continue. This is not solely because he is 'weak', 'sinful' and anxious for 'a good time'. Most people get a fair amount of fun out of their lives, but, on balance, life is suffering and only the very young or the very foolish imagine otherwise.'

Milly and many another dog would certainly not agree with the creator of *Animal Farm*. She has a high old time every day of the year. Life reaches its peak when she is given the chance to round up sheep and its nadir when she is told to go to bed – a procedure which she considers to be completely pointless. With human beings, of course, it is different. We are more complicated, less easy to please. One man, who would certainly have disagreed with Orwell, was Tom Parker, one of England's great instinctive farmers, who was a ploughboy at twelve years old and lived to own and cultivate thousands of Hampshire's finest acres. Across the south country he was known as The Guv'nor and he was admired and respected far and wide. As well as being generous and the best of good company, he was a tough and ruthless man. He said that he had been forced to be that way – otherwise he would have gone under. He had a spring in his step, even in his eighties, and he used to say that the fertile land which he farmed was just a breeding-ground for rabbits when he first started out. He was a fine old man, straight

Tom Parker – 'The Guv'nor'

of back and strong of limb and his stern, commanding eyes harked back to a time when leaders led and no questions were asked. When I first got to know him, he was a multi-millionaire driving his Rolls Royce across the corn stubble. One of his many cheerful stories – told in his rich, southern voice – came from the turn of the twentieth century when he was a child in the north of the county which he loved so well:- 'I was born in March, 1896, and we had a system in the countryside in those days. Not all the men had very large farms. In our village there was a man with a bigger farm than the others and he kept our local bull. Or another kept the boar. Someone else had the ram. And in the same way the shepherds bred their sheepdogs. It was just our custom, going back through the generations. And that bull was used by everybody in the parish, and so was the boar and the tup. In some hamlets they used to go and get the sow and take her to the boar, when needs be, and in other cases they used to take the ram to the ewes. It just depended on the circumstances. And that was the way it went in our parish. Well, old Mrs Greene wanted to see Mr Thompson, lives down the other end of the village. Along she goes, raps on the door and out comes Mrs Thompson.

Mrs Green says, 'Is Mr Thompson in?'

No he wasn't. What a pity.

Mrs Thompson asks, 'What do you want, anyway?'

'I just want a loan of his ear.'

'What about?'

'I just want a word with him.'

Mrs Thompson tells her, 'Well, he's gone to market. So you can't see him.'

'When will he be home?'

'He'll be home very late', the old lady says. 'And what is it you want anyway – 'cos I know all about the farm. If it's the boar you want, its 7/6d; if it's the bull you want, it's a guinea.'

Mrs Green replies, 'It's not about either – it's about the state of me daughter.'

'Oh my God,' says Mrs Thompson, 'then you will have to see him yourself, because I couldn't tell you what he would charge you.'

And she shut the door in her face.'

The Guv'nor's laugh echoed round the yard as he finished – the sight and sound of a man who had managed to deal with most of the mysteries and miseries of life with skill and success.

Another memorable countryman whom I came to know in my film-making days was Jack Lewis from Balcombe in Sussex. He was a dog fanatic and would have been a good friend to my Milly with his small pack of impeccably behaved retrievers. He never rose to the dizzy heights which Tom Parker achieved, but he knew every inch of the landscape in which he rejoiced to live and was wise in the ways of plants and animals. Jack died in his eightieth year on the night of 8th December 1985. He was buried a few

Jack Lewis, Sussex gamekeeper and village elder at Balcombe

Jack Lewis and his family and friends at Bowders Farm with two of his retrievers

days later on a wet and blustery day in the old churchyard. Most of the village turned out to say goodbye. Jack's knowledge and experience of country ways and country moods was broad and full of wisdom and he and his family formed a core of those who helped to maintain village life in the old style. He was a tall, upright old man with the ginger in his hair only just beginning to fade. That colour gave warning that there might be a temper beneath the warm-hearted and hospitable exterior. And certainly there was strength and power in everything that he did. The north country accent remained, though it had mellowed through years of contact with soft southerners. The eyes were shrewd and summed up strangers swiftly. Jack was seldom rude to fools, knaves or sycophants, but he saw through them

36

quickly and intuitively. Strong and fit right up to the end, he died in his bed as he would have wished on a cold winter's night with his three beloved golden retrievers around him.

Snow came to Balcombe during the January of Jack's last year. First thing every morning and several times each day the old man marched out through the blizzards and the ice to feed the flocks of ducks, geese, pheasants, chickens, guinea fowl, peacocks and peahens, as well as the swarms of small garden birds, which treated his home in their hundreds as a hospitable sanctuary. Dressed in heavy-duty clothes, he looked like a throw-back to the middle ages, a stalwart peasant farmer. And the birds, in their hunger, showed no fear of him or of his impeccably trained dogs: 'When it snows there's a bewildered expression on them. They don't know what it is. And it takes days and days for them to get used to it. It affects them in several ways, but I think the main thing is that they take it for granted that they are far better off sitting where they are than worrying and looking for grub. I think they accept it better than we do. I feed so many for so long. I don't think I can do any more. The majority of birds around here will come to where I am. I have not got to go and look for them. If they know there is a food supply, distance doesn't matter. If you clear a space in an acre of ground and put some grain down they will come to it. They find a way to pass on the information and they manage to tell one another.' As he speaks a new flight of ducks sails in through the snowflakes. They waddle forwards self-importantly and begin to help themselves.

It is not just the birds which suffer in cold weather. All living creatures have urgent and often unexpected problems. As Jack puts it, 'I was farm manager at one time and I had some cattle, ten heifers and a bull, in a field. And it was terrible weather. I went out one morning and there were icicles on them. It had snowed and thawed and then it had frozen up again, and the icicles were under the belly – some of them a foot long. I didn't know what to do. So I made a shed out of tin and put some barley straw into it. But those cows would not go into it. Why? I don't know. The only time they used the building was in the summer to get out of the way of the flies. And they laid out on the open field in that freezing, windy weather. And every morning they had these icicles on them.'

It is probably no exaggeration to say that Jack's three best friends were his dogs. I can certainly boast that I have no friend like Milly. Human visitors regularly came to his cottage and always found a cup of tea or a meal and a warm welcome. The old man walked the dogs as though they were athletes in training and fed them like champions. For a special treat he had them lie on their backs and then scratched their tummies with a birch besom. In return he expected good manners and instant obedience. He also received a non-stop abundance of affection. One of his favourite walks was along the side of a meadow with glistening Balcombe reservoir as a backdrop. Ancient oaks grow in the rich pasture and the old man strode out, walking stick in hand, with his tweed hat low on his forehead. Around his feet the dogs side-stepped and jostled, each in search of the favoured position at his heel.

Jack worked as gamekeeper on the local estate, so the dogs were an essential part of his job. After his retirement his son, John, took over from him. But his father still loved to go out with his senior retriever, Angus, during the shooting days to help find the wounded birds, to join in with the work of the beaters and to enjoy the cheerful company. It is classic game-bird shooting country in this part of Sussex with steep banks, thick cover, wide open arable fields and broad rides through woodland. The guns travel in a farm trailer, sitting on bales and with a tarpaulin cover to protect them from the worst of the weather. The beaters move slowly through the woods, their cries echoing round the trees and scaring the pheasants into flight. And the dogs are on the move on all sides – tense, excited and longing for action: 'It's their nature to hunt and to catch things, isn't it? Why does a fox like hunting a rabbit? He really loves it. And when he's caught it he'll throw it up in the air and gloat over it. I have seen them doing that many times. When they catch hold of a pheasant they're like that too and they will play with it unless they are very hungry. The first thing they do then is to eat it. Sometimes it's the same thing with a dog. They were once wild and they've been tamed by human beings and we've taught them. We could train a fox in the same way if we went to the trouble. And you can discipline a dog without being cruel in any way. All this hitting dogs and shouting at them or spoiling them is useless. But they will do almost anything for kindness. And if you understand them and go into their lives, you'll find that they're much cleverer than they're given credit for. They're certainly a notch or two up on some humans I know.'

Jack gently fondled the ears of the little one, the least obedient of the three. And she looked up at him as though she wished she could die for him at that moment. Milly sometimes looks at me like that, if I am lucky, when I go to say goodnight to her where she sleeps in our downstairs bathroom. Jack went on: 'I'll give you an instance of how dogs are just as intelligent as people. I was digging in my garden, quite a long way from the house. Now I am growing a bit deaf in my old age but I heard the dog howling. So I put the spade down and came to the back door and the telephone was ringing. I answered it and the man said that he had been hanging on for ages. So I told him that I was sorry, that I had been in the garden and that I hadn't heard it. Two or three days after, the same thing happened again. I was splitting logs for the fire when I heard the dogs hollering. So in I came and the phone was ringing. Now this little dog, if I am not indoors and if the telephone goes off, she'll come to the door and shout. She doesn't bark. She just howls. I think it's wonderful. So now I'm sure I could train that dog to do or to tell me practically anything. Obviously, how it's come about, I've been sitting indoors, the telephone's rung and I've jumped up. I always try to answer it quickly, because you never know if it's an emergency. The dogs have all jumped up as well and we've gone to the telephone together. So when I've not been there, the little dog has thought, 'Well, I'd better do something about this'. And she has.'

The moon rides high in the clear sky, promising fine days ahead. Bowder's Cottage sits warm and cosy on its small rise, one window winking back at the moon. Jack, in contemplative mood, was sitting by the fire. The strong, old head leant back against the worn cloth of the armchair: 'Can you tell me of anything that wants to die? Animals, human beings, everything wants to live. Everything I've ever met wants to live, unless it's a nutcase, whether it's been well-treated or ill-treated. That is why some poor people who have got a dreadful illness get over it. The want to live overrules the trouble. I've seen animals go through the most terrible things. When I was a young keeper there was an old man cutting some grass for hay with two horses and a mowing machine. I was going up the hedge with my gun and he shouted across to me, 'Here. Come here, young chap. I've just cut a hen pheasant. Look, I've gone and cut her legs off and she's flown away into the wood.' She'd left ten eggs there in the grass. So he pulled the horses on a bit and left a piece of the grass uncut, covering the eggs. And I went along the next day, when the old carter had finished his job, and I had a look and the hen pheasant was back on her nest. And I made a point of going and looking every day and I saw that pheasant for weeks and weeks. She reared six young ones. And she only had the two stumps, so we christened her Stumpy. And she brought up her little ones somehow. It wants some doing, but she managed it.'

When I asked Jack Lewis how he would like to be remembered, he chuckled and the handsome face screwed up and the eyes twinkled, 'I know how I'll be remembered,' he said, 'as a cantankerous old bugger.' Let it be his epitaph for that extraordinary, old man would not have felt easy about his praises being sung.

MILLY thinks that chess is boring. She tells me, I believe, that, if she set her mind to it, she could be a grand master – or should that be mistress? But there are far more interesting things to be involved with, like the sheep and the hens and the visiting badger. I am intrigued by the parable of the man from India who is said to have invented that infuriating, brain-stretching and intricate contest. The prince, for whom the work had been done, was so enchanted with the game of chess that he offered the inventor any reward that he wished to receive to thank him for his genius. The man thought for a moment and then told his master that he would like to have one grain of rice on the first of the sixty-four squares – two on the second, four on the third, eight on the fourth, and so on up to sixty-four. This seemed a small enough request. So it was granted. The catch for the boss was that, mathematically, by the time you get half-way – to number thirty-two – you will have rice for six elephants to carry. After that the quantity increases exponentially until, by the time you reach the last square on the chess board, you have a pile of rice larger than Mount Everest – more than has been produced so far in the history of the world. It would take the brain which invented one of the planet's most sophisticated and complicated puzzles to work that one out.

Fortunately for him, this inventor pleased his employer. And just as well too. Failure to give satisfaction in those dark and distant days could lead to a sentence of death or, at least, to a long spell behind bars. When I first met Milly her home was a three-foot by two-foot barred cage in a small council house. Her owner worked nights at the nearby supermarket. His partner was on the day shift. They also had two small children. So Milly failed to get the exercise she wanted, even though she was much loved. She spent a great deal of time in her small gaol cell. Outside the house were concrete walkways with metal handrails. Close at hand was a litter-strewn, muddy football pitch where she used to go for a run. I find it hard to see animals caged – even if it is sometimes necessary. It is more difficult still to come to terms with human beings in prison, although many may have deserved their punishment.

One of the hobbies which Elisabeth and I share is to visit men in prison. We travel quite widely – to Usk in Wales, to the Isle of Sheppey in Kent, to Wandsworth in London, to Leicestershire and to Oxford. It is a fascinating and sometimes heart-breaking task. We have met some of the best people in prison cells and some of the nastiest. Among the guards there are a few saints. There are also men who would have fitted well into the Nazi system at Auschwitz. One of these asked me why I wasted my time coming to see these bad men. Why did I not, instead, go and visit his lonely old mother, who had never done an evil deed in her life and who would love to have a visitor? I regret that I had no answer for him. Some things in life are impossible to explain. There are many laughs and quite a few tears when you are talking to people behind the high walls of one of Her Majesty's prisons. A while back I was sitting in a cell on C Wing at Winchester Prison. I was with a burglar, a murderer, a money-launderer and a man who was in for committing grievous bodily harm. The conversation was lively, mainly because all four men were smoking spliffs. They kept on asking me to have a look out onto the wing to see if one of the screws might be coming past. I told them that, if a guard arrived in the cell, there would be no doubt about what was going on because it was barely possible to see across the room for smoke. Later, when I got back to my car, I had to sit for an hour with the window open doing deep breathing exercises. I could not drive because of all the second-hand marijuana smoke, which I had inhaled. One thing I am sure of from my years of prison visiting – many of the men, though certainly not all of them, should be running free like Milly in the meadows. Some might need tagging, but the waste of life and of colossal sums of public money, which are involved in keeping tens of thousands of people locked up, is a national tragedy. It surely cannot be beyond the wit of man to find something more sensible to do with those who present no danger to the public and who could, like my dear dog, do something useful and fulfilling with their lives.

My most treasured sensation of undiluted freedom comes in the early spring when I harrow and then roll our seventeen acres of meadows. I hitch up our red, 1959 Massey Ferguson tractor to the tangled tines of the veteran implement and drag it to and fro and round and round the grassland. What finer feeling on earth can there be than sitting on the bouncing seat, the engine growling away, the cool sun overhead, the jingle-jangle music of the metal dragged behind, a collie dog trotting along for company, buzzards floating in the thermals, pheasants pecking in the hedgerows and short-stalked, wild daffodils lighting up the carpet of the two-acre wood. The elation which I feel during these precious days is beyond my powers of description. But, if you want to experience ultimate freedom, it is what I would recommend. The power hunger and viciousness of civil servants and politicians fades away into insignificance. The blackmail based on the use of guilt and the hypocrisy of the clergy cease to matter. And the crookery and greed and stupidity of the bankers and the other money men find a proper perspective. My anger at all these abuses vanishes and is replaced by a calm happiness, which no one can remove – not even the great and the good. As Hemingway might have written – I spit in the semen of their grandfathers.

The reason for harrowing and rolling our fields is nearly the same as the motive for combing your hair. It certainly makes them look more presentable after the onslaught of the winter months. It allows the air into the topsoil, tears out the clumps of dead grass, undoes the damage of molehills and badger grubbing and scatters dead leaves and twigs. It is satisfying to look at the pasture land after the harrow has done its work and then again after it has been rolled. The patterns are different but equally pleasing. Some farmers roll as soon as they have finished harrowing. I like to leave it for a few days in the hope of a shower or two of rain. I have an old-fashioned view that the land does not like to be hurried.

We had a dear friend called Alice Spinney, who shared that belief. She was a proper shepherd and ran two thousand ewes on the Wiltshire Downs – an enormous undertaking. If you imagine taking care of all those feet and worming all those stomachs and then you take into account the pressure times of lambing and shearing, you can understand that Alice earned her keep every week of the year. Her sheep were Speckled Faced Beulahs from Wales – hill and mountain animals and wild as stags. We bought some of them from her and bred them for more than ten years until they became too big and boisterous for our weary, old limbs and we switched to a smaller, calmer breed. Somehow Alice managed to spare the time to make the one and half hour journey every year to help us with shearing. If we had a problem she was always ready to speak on the telephone or even to travel

Alice Spinney

over to the New Forest. She was a modern day saint and a most practical and professional one. Though she would have loved my Milly, her sheepdogs were from New Zealand. They were, big, husky chaps, which relied on their bark and their bulk to get these huge flocks on the move in the required direction, whereas Milly uses her cunning and her speed. One bleak, mid-winter's day Alice was out alone feeding her animals on the steep downland. She had often spoken about how dangerous these slopes were for shepherds on quad bikes. She preferred the safety of her trusty old tractor and trailer. She jumped down from the cab to open a gate, leading into one of the pastures. While she was working on the gate-chain the tractor rolled forward and pinned her to the post. She had not pulled on the hand brake hard enough. She took a long time to die out there in the bitter wind and cold. Sherborne Abbey was packed when we gathered to say goodbye to this special friend on 9th January 2004. She was thirty-eight years old. Her two young children lit and carried giant candles. Then this wonderful farewell, written by an unknown poet, ushered her to her grave:

> 'Do not stand at my grave and weep;
> I am not there, I do not sleep.
> I am a thousand winds that blow.
> I am the diamond glints on snow.
> I am the sunlight on ripened grain.
> I am the gentle autumn rain.
> When you awaken in the morning's hush
> I am the swift, uplifting rush
> Of quiet birds in circled flight.
> I am the soft stars that shine at night.
> Do not stand at my grave and cry.
> I am not there. I did not die.'

They do not build many like Alice Spinney in our modern world, which seems to be obsessed with disability benefits and social security and rights without responsibilities. And the more is the pity. She was an honest and skilled worker. She would have viewed with amazement our political leaders cheating on their expenses, our trough-gulping bankers and our sly and dishonest permanent secretaries. Thank God that there are a few folk such as her to keep alive the flicker of hope that there is still some vestige of decency, justice and fairness in this once great land of ours.

I am unclear about Milly's view of death, though I am certain that she and Alice would have been the best of friends if they had overlapped and that Milly would have missed Alice as much as we do. What I can vouch for is that Milly enjoys our local graveyard at Minstead, where we go on Wednesday mornings to mow and strim and tidy and to try to catch moles. She loves hunting and exploring around the gravestones and the novelty and variety of the location. Our granddaughter, Maisy, lies buried here. She died, aged ten weeks, on 26th April in the year 2000 and is guarded by an angel, carved from Portland stone, whose small head I pat whenever I pass by. Close at hand is the grave of Conan Doyle, the creator of Sherlock Holmes, Dr Watson and Moriarty. He was first buried in Sussex. As a spiritualist he was standing upright in his grave there. Later, his widow, who lived in nearby Brook, arranged for him to be moved to Minstead, where he now lies beside her. Whether his spirit is troubled by this posthumous change of position is anyone's guess, though the oak tree beside the grave is said to have been struck twice by lightning.

Often we overlap at the churchyard with the cheerful bunch of young men – and sometimes women – from the Community Payback Scheme. They work hard and effectively and make a huge difference to the look of the place. Would that more of the men whom we know behind prison bars could be allowed to be punished in this way rather than wasting their time and taxpayers' millions behind prison walls. These youngsters are interested in Maisy and in Conan Doyle – and of course in Milly as well. But their greatest joy is in the grave of villager, Thomas White, by the size and grandeur of his stone a pillar of the local community in the middle of the nineteenth century. All the usual compliments are carved into the memorial – loved father and grandfather, churchwarden, lay preacher and so on. Once upon a time the words 'faithful husband' were also included. But, soon after his death, his widow had the 'faithful' carefully chiselled out, so that it now just reads 'husband'. She obviously discovered that he had not been true to her. The young people are pleased to discover that they are not the only ones who have strayed off the straight and narrow path. Perish the thought, but even the great and the good sometimes give into temptation. It is hard to credit, I know, but it seems to be so.

Sheep used to graze the rich grass of Minstead churchyard, as they had done since mediaeval times, keeping it trim and neat and tidy. It was a perfect, pastoral scene to arrive there and to find half-a-dozen ewes doing the work that we try to do today and achieving it rather more effectively and usefully than we possibly can. After all, they were there twenty-four hours a day and, as a result of the excellent pasture, produced top-notch lamb for Sunday lunch after the morning service. Then some local busybodies complained about sheep manure on the graves. It is hard to believe but that is what happens when townspeople come into the countryside. They always know best. They always interfere. They should stay in the smell and the smoke of the city. Today, alas, the sheep have gone, banished by ignorance and urban fastidiousness.

Visitors come from all over the world to Minstead, not just because it is a beautiful place in the heart of the New Forest but also to visit the resting place of Sir Arthur Conan Doyle. It is a welcome break for me, in the middle of mowing or setting mole traps, to take people to his grave and to rehearse yet again my well-worn routine. So it was no surprise when, one perfect, summer's morning, a young gentleman with an American accent approached me and asked if I could help him. I was pleased to do so and took him straight to the Sherlock Holmes grave. That was fine, he told me, but it was not why he had come. He had travelled all the way from Boston, where he was a bassoon and serpent player with the Symphony Orchestra there, to find one of the two graves in this country with a serpent carved into the headstone. For those, like me, who are ignorant, a serpent, as well as being a snake, is a rare musical instrument. I was nonplussed. In all my years of weeding, clearing anthills and tidying up I had never seen this memorial. After a painstaking search we found it. The nineteenth century grave belonged to a band member of a great Hampshire regiment, one of whose instruments was the serpent – and there it was cut carefully into the stone with every sinuous coil complete. The American then asked if I could do him one more favour. He went to his car and came back with his camera and with his own musical instrument, beautifully covered in python skin. He stood by the grave with the mouth-piece up to his lips and I took his photograph. Then he took the deepest of deep breaths and began to play, '*Lead kindly light amid the encircling gloom. Lead thou me on.*' It was a magic moment. It is not hard to say that it was more tuneful than my amateur church bell ringing efforts, but it was also the best and most moving music that I have heard at our much-loved church.

Milly does not like snakes or serpents. I think that she is afraid of them – though I would not say that in front of her. Nor does she much like maybugs or stag beetles or any large creepy crawlies. I have never yet seen her in a confrontation with a snake, but I sense that she would be a coward. Again, I would not talk about it in her presence, but I once saw her giving a wide berth to a small slow-worm. As for me, I have no strong feelings about these creatures, though I was once bitten by an adder in Scotland. So I treat them, as one should all living things, with a certain respect. I was fishing in a burn for brown trout for our supper and walked along a rough track beside the stream searching for one of those black pools with a waterfall tumbling into it, where the watchful fish lurk and feed. The vertical bank on my right beside the path rose six feet and more above my head. The adder, unseen by me, was sunning himself on a ledge at shoulder height. The passage was narrow, so I must have brushed against him as I passed and frightened him. He hit me hard on the biceps with his fangs. My thin shirt offered no protection. No help was at hand. I could not reach the wound with my mouth to try to suck out the poison and I could not get at the place with my left hand and my pen knife to attempt a bit of useless surgery. So I sat down on the bank of the river, feeling sore and a little sick, waiting for whatever was going to happen. Nothing much did. So after an hour of wasted fishing time I went on my way, had a naked swim and rubbed my shoulder in the icy water and then, if I remember it right, caught a couple of decent fish for high tea.

In my limited experience hornets are more dangerous than adders. One late spring at our forester's cottage they started to build a nest in the roof of one of our small stables. As summer took over we watched with fascination while the nest and the numbers grew. They were private and independent insects and seemed to be entirely uninterested in us. We treated them with deference, were happy to have them as neighbours and were careful not to disturb or frighten them as they went about their daily business. In August I began to paint the outside of our house. It is not my favourite task and it is important not to attempt to do too much in one session or in an hour or in a week. Slow and steady wins the day. The paint is kept in the hornets' stable. So, whenever my bucket ran dry, I climbed down the ladder and went to get a refill. At lunchtime I was topping up the can to be ready for my last onslaught of the day. Suddenly and for no reason that I could understand, the gentle humming from the nest in the rafters turned into an angry roar and the spitfires came in to attack me. I ran for the house spilling half a gallon of good paint as I fled. By some miracle I only received two stings in the back before I slammed the kitchen door on the pursuing bad guys. This time I felt distinctly groggy and took a day or two to recover. It gave me a good excuse to take a break from the painting, which was useful enough. But I still do not know what caused them to attack me. Perhaps it was the smell of my sweaty body – enough to annoy any living creature.

In the 1950s when I was in my twenties I was fortunate enough to be invited to go on an Amazon expedition. Now there was a place for monster bugs and frightening creatures of every shape and size. Sometimes a cattle owner had to be paid to drive one of his old, dry cows into a tributary upstream of where we were going to ford. This was so that the piranha fish would rush through the water for a free and easy meal while we crossed in relative safety without having our toes nibbled. Mostly we overnighted in spartan, Brazilian army camps. When we walked into these dormitories there was sometimes a sound like half-a-dozen people scrumpling up newspaper pages. This was caused by thousands of cockroaches scurrying away across the floor and over the ceiling. One morning, when I went to have an early, cold-water shower there, straddling the plug-hole, was the biggest spider I have seen, glaring up at me. I decided to remain dirty and smelly that day.

When we came to Manaus, that famous city with its beautiful opera house, nearly two thousand miles up the great river from its mouth at Belem, we found the barracks in which we were going to spend the next three nights. I was allocated the top berth in a triple-layered bunk. This meant that I lay within a couple of feet of the ceiling. There was a gap of a foot between the top of the dormitory wall and the roof of the building. This was to permit the air to circulate in the furious heat and humidity of the rain forest. It also allowed flying creatures of all shapes and sizes easy access. Now there were no cupboards, chairs, tables or wash bowls in this room. So, at the foot of my bed, I had to stow my rucksack, my clothes, my metal heeled boots and my precious torch and penknife. There was no electricity. I was exhausted and soon slept – naked as usual because of the heat. I awoke in the pitch black and realised straight away that something large and with several legs was sitting in the middle of my chest. I was not pleased about this. I reached down slowly and gingerly with my left hand to where I knew I had put my trusty boots, gripped one of them firmly by the toe, raised it as high as possible in my cramped situation and whacked it down as hard as I could onto my chest. I felt something large catapult away off my body and over the edge of the bed. Relief. I reached for my torch, switched it on and surveyed the scene, trying at the same time not to awaken my sleeping companions. There was blood everywhere. My right hand was dripping with it and there was an ugly gash on the back of it. During the night I had lain on my right arm. It had gone to sleep and it was numb and had lost all feeling. What had been lying on my chest was my own right hand and not a monstrous tarantula as I had feared and imagined. In my stupidity, I had dealt myself a grievous wound. I have come across self-harming in my time but that was carrying it to a ridiculous extreme.

ON the whole, Milly is good around the house and about the garden. I only have to whisper the words 'On your bed,' and she goes straight to her cushion in the downstairs bathroom and lies down. On Monday mornings, when we do housework, she knows that she must be outside while Elisabeth dusts, cleans and tidies downstairs and I do my bit in the relatively easy upstairs rooms and on the staircase. When I am mowing our half-acre of lawn, Milly trots up and down beside me until she gets bored. Then she disappears for a while to mooch around in the bushes before returning for another stint of duty. Whenever I switch the engine off to empty the bin she rushes up to me because it is she who decides whether this batch of grass clippings will go onto the compost heap or into the run for the hens to kick around and to peck. That is one explanation for the golden yellow of our egg yolks. Milly will lead me to whichever destination she feels has the greater need. I almost always obey her because she is put out if I do not. On Saturday mornings, before we set out to do our weekly food shopping, I fill up the water for the chickens and clean out their wooden hut, giving them new straw laced with tick powder. Milly, helpful as ever, guards the entrance to the hut to stop the birds coming in while I am scraping the floor planks and tidying the inside. She takes this job seriously and glowers and sometimes snaps and snarls if any hen dares to set foot on the ladder leading up to the narrow entrance while I am at work inside.

Four times a year I clean out the gutters round our house and around the outbuildings. This is a serious job and quite challenging for a seventy-five year old with a dodgy left knee. The highest place I need to reach is probably twenty-five feet from the ground, and I have to climb up and down our ancient, extended ladder more than a dozen times to complete the task. As always, Milly is to the fore and bustles about full of her normal self-importance. As I come down to earth she greets me with a furiously wagging tail and like a long lost friend and, as I climb up again, she watches anxiously from below and seems to be saying that I am too old to be doing this and that surely I could teach her how. Then, with a shrug, she puts her paws on the bottom rung as though she is trying to stop the ladder slipping. And one day, I fear, that is exactly what it will do in spite of her best efforts. No matter. I have always felt contempt for the health and safety brigade and for their absurd rules and regulations.

The other morning I was asleep, as one should be, at 3.30 am. Elisabeth jerked me awake with a whispered, 'Chickens', in my right ear. This happens quite regularly in our lives as smallholders. And it means that action is called for. Hens do not cluck in the dark. If they do start muttering there is danger afoot – a fox, a badger, a stray dog on the rampage. And my wife, whose hearing is keener than mine, had been woken up by sounds from the chicken hutch – just fifteen yards down from our bedroom window. We have a well-rehearsed routine. Elisabeth goes to the spare room window and starts

Milly, AH, and a broody Light Sussex hen

rattling the metal bar, which holds it open, and shouting at the intruder. I rush downstairs with Elisabeth close behind me, grab a torch and whatever weapon I can find and run out of the back door. There is no purpose in taking a gun when it is pitch dark. Milly and Ted, our daughter's city slicker of a dog, who was a house guest at the time, dash out with me, all agog, into the cold night. I get to the chicken run. The hens are out and frantic with worry. I shine the torch round the tall, netting enclosure. Nothing. Then I hear a sound from the chicken hutch behind me. I turn and shine the beam of the torch onto the entrance and a badger's head peeps out at me. There is blood on his mouth and I can see the savaged body of one of our beautiful Light Sussex hens lying motionless behind him. He ducks back in. I snatch a garden spade which Elisabeth has brought out with her, and hand her the torch. The badger eventually makes his exit, blinded by the glare. Elisabeth, steady as a rock, holds him in the torchlight. It reminds me of the searchlights during the war hunting the German bombers on their way back from London over the farm where I grew up in Suffolk. I do my grim duty with the spade. It is not an easy or a quick job to kill a wild animal without a knife or a gun. At last it is over and silence restored. I look up to see the two dogs from outside the run watching me aghast and with wide-eyed amazement. The chicken will not have died in vain – it will make a fine Sunday lunch. The badger's coat might be turned into a warm jacket. If we are adventurous we could even try cooking his hams. The village must wonder what the hubbub on the hill is all about.

I am told that I am not allowed to kill a badger. I hear that I can be sent to prison for two years and fined a fortune if I do. But I am unrepentant. I think that they are fine-looking animals. But they are not the cuddly toys, which so many town people imagine – and there are far too many of them. They are ferocious, carnivorous beasts and need to be controlled. I am unafraid to say that, if they are going to torment and kill my hens, I am going to have my revenge by one means or another. I have seen a fair amount of death in my time. The slaughter man comes to our house each year to dispatch our sheep. It is not my favourite day but it has to be done. It never ceases to astonish me how tough animals are. On our way to visit our friends in Winchester prison a couple of years ago, the car in front of us crashed

Badger – friend or foe?

into a fallow deer, which was trotting across the road in the dusk. The collision shattered the animal's right shoulder and it was pirouetting frantically in the road unable to make any forward progress. It was mortally wounded. They werc townspeople in the car. They stood on the pavement appalled, their hands up to their mouths and tears in their eyes. I grabbed the poor beast and, strong though it was, managed to wrestle it to the sidewalk so that the all-important and impatient traffic could start to flow again. Citizens looked at me out of their car windows as though I was some kind of a murderer. The deer needed to be killed. It had to be put out of its pain and fear. I had no knife or gun with me. So I begged one of the onlookers to go to a house and ask for a carving knife from the people who lived there so that I could cut the animal's throat. Meanwhile I was trying with all my might and in vain to strangle it. At long last a police car rolled up and together we managed to do what was needed. It took a horribly long time. As I stood there with the borrowed carving knife in my hand, one of the policeman said to me, 'You had better get rid of that sharpish or I shall have to arrest you.' I took it back to its owner and we drove on to the relative sanity of Her Majesty's Prison in Winchester. I do not remember anyone offering me a word of thanks. Nor do I wish for it – just one of life's ugly duties when you have the good fortune to live and to learn in the English countryside.

That most unlikely Etonian, George Orwell, wrote in *Politics and the English language*, 'In our time, political speech and writing are largely the defence of the indefensible.' And so it is today. Milly does not love or respect or admire the busybody bureaucrats of Brussels or Strasbourg – or of Whitehall, come to that. Nor does her master. I voted 'No' in the 1975 referendum on Europe against that master of deceit, prime minister Heath – the grotesque Grocer. I shall vote 'No' again in 2017 in the unlikely event that promises are kept and that I am given the chance. What are the solemn undertakings of politicians worth? Nothing at all – less than nothing. Yet, being half-Greek and half-English, I love the countries of Europe and their peoples – Greece and Cyprus, of course, which I know well. Italy, France, where we ski most winters, Spain, Germany and Romania. I could go on. What I detest are the civil servants and the power-hungry mediocrities at the heart of the spider's web. We have an acquaintance, who was an employee of the British Foreign Office, seconded on a fine salary with an insanely generous pension scheme to the European Commission. At our expense he lived in a spacious villa by Lake Como in Italian Lombardy. At our expense he was driven in chauffeured splendour to his four-day week in Brussels or Strasbourg, depending on which city was sheltering the madhouse that month. At our expense he sailed a handsome yacht on the lake's blue waters. At our expense his children were educated at British public schools. At our expense he skied most three-day winter weekends in the mountains. And like many another not-so-noble, now ennobled British labour and conservative Commissioner, he made a habit of taking his limousine and driver to the best restaurants with his family and personal friends to wine and dine them – all at our great expense. Are we really meant to believe that we are lucky to be a part of such a charade? And it is no better here at home in Westminster. As I write, in April 2013, it is reported that out of the 635 MPs in our majestic House of Commons:-

29 have been accused of abusing their husbands or wives

7 have been arrested for fraud

9 are being investigated for writing bad cheques

17 have directly or indirectly bankrupted at least two businesses

3 have done prison time for assault

71 cannot get a credit card due to bad debts

14 have been arrested on drug-related charges

8 have been detained for shoplifting

21 are currently defendants in law suits

84 have been arrested for drink/driving in the last 12 months.

Yes, really! Collectively, in the last year alone, these creatures have cost the British taxpayer £92,993,748 in expenses – and we all know what that means. This is the same bunch of people who, each session, churn out scores of new rules and regulations designed to keep the rest of us on the straight and narrow. And, just to add insult to grievous injury, they have voted themselves one of the greediest corporate pension schemes in the country.

Milly and I both like adventures – not every day but at regular intervals. Some of them I can write about. Some of them I definitely cannot. Within easy range in our beloved Forest there is plenty happening, in spite of the fact that city people seem to think that country life is boring. It is not. There is as much mischief and excitement and skulduggery going on in our part of Hampshire as any man or dog could wish for. Alas, one of my occasional enterprises involves the heart-break of leaving Milly behind. It means driving across Europe to Romania to deliver much-needed medical supplies to a hospital in the town of Zalau close to the border with Ukraine. Milly would hate the long journey, for she is not a car dog. So I have to bid her a tearful farewell and set out for the Channel ports without her. We drive through Belgium, past the hypocrisy and corruption that is Brussels, and on into Germany where we overnight on the hospitable floor of an eighty-year-old couple in the East. All that they ask is that we take them some English marmalade. The next day we follow the beauty of the Danube across Hungary and into Budapest, where we are the guests of a bunch of jolly nuns in their welcoming convent. And on day three we cross the border into Romania, hopefully without incident, and come to our destination. Our quarters there are in the town museum where we sleep and dream surrounded rather eerily by suits of armour, stern-faced statues and a yawning sarcophagus. Zalau, with its ferocious pot-holed streets, still carries many of the scars of the twenty-two year rule of Nicolae Ceausescu and his witch of a wife, Elena. But its people today are warm and hospitable to strangers, the hospital is overwhelmingly grateful for the modest goods that we bring, many of which have passed their sell-by dates in England. And the nearby wooden, country churches are buildings of exquisite beauty and fascination. And then there are the magnificent Roman remains, entirely unsullied by tourism and litter, and the scattered villages of the Romany gypsies. The streets in these hamlets are ankle-deep in mud and sewage and the depth of poverty is palpable. You do not ask people if they are unemployed. You enquire if they have ever worked or had a job. Everywhere there are huge and savage dogs. I am not a man of great courage, but I do not usually fear dogs. These ones are different. They make Milly look like a puppy. They mean business and their owners do not seem to be interested in stopping them from doing their worst. We have had many close encounters of the canine kind.

The other day I was driving our tractor across our 'fallen tree' field. I was dragging a big roller behind me to smooth out and press down the land after the harrow and the fertiliser spreader had done their good work. Our own small flock of Gotland sheep – seven of them pregnant ewes – were quietly grazing in the meadow where I was working. As I was turning at the end of a run, I looked over the fence into our neighbour's field and there was a huge, brown dog – the spitting image of the Romanian gypsy brutes – chasing his sheep and lambs and trying to grab hold of them. They were running for their lives. If I had had my gun with me I would have tried to shoot the beast. But I did not. There is no space for baggage of that kind on these old tractors. I turned off the engine, remembered to jam on the hand-brake – otherwise the weight of the roller would have dragged everything swiftly down the hill to destruction – and ran, shouting curses at the top of my voice, as fast as my old legs would carry me. As best I could manage I clambered over the barbed wire, ripping my boiler suit on the way. By now the dog had the sheep cornered in the yard. By the mercy of God our neighbour's wife had heard the barking, the shouting and the commotion and had come out to the gate. Together we managed to protect the lambs from the attack. I tried in vain to lay hold of the dog. But he was too quick and strong for me. He looked like an Alsatian crossed with a lurcher. At last he cantered away and disappeared into the wood beside the field. It was then that, for the first time, I heard the owner's voice calling. In my fury I shouted back, using language that I should not have employed in front of a woman. The invisible stranger said that he was sorry. 'Not as sorry you would have bloody well been if I had had my gun with me,' I replied. People should learn to keep their dogs on a lead if they cannot control them when there are sheep or other animals about. I have seen half-a dozen ewes savaged beyond repair by a dog, whose owner should have known better. Such tragedies are avoidable. And where was Milly during all this drama – an adventure which she would have relished? She was at home keenly awaiting the arrival of Chris, the postman. It was probably just as well, because I cannot easily imagine what part she would have played in this exhausting episode.

During my working years as a film and television director I did not devote too much of my life to sheep or to Welsh border collies, though quite a lot of my time was spent on location in the splendour of the English countryside in all its moods and seasons. My concentration in those distant days was more likely to be on projects like the re-introduction of *Dick Barton Special*

Agent to the silver screen, trying to get Dusty Springfield to remember her lines and positions, wrestling with the intellect of Diana Dors, the America's Cup from Fremantle in Western Australia or classical music concerts from Penshurst Place in Sussex. If it is true in television that the talented specialise, you can draw your own conclusions from that short list about my modest skills. As a callow producer of twenty-five years old I decided one day, for reasons which now elude me, to include a small flock of sheep in a studio show with an audience. It was a crazy idea at its conception. It should have been snuffed out then. A score or so of mature lambs do not mix well on a shiny studio floor with cameras, cables, lights and microphone booms – let alone with a bunch of excited men and women. That the original 'inspiration' became a reality is the stuff of the lunatic asylum. If ever there was an occasion when I needed the help and wisdom of my dear friend Milly this was it. The day of the broadcast arrived – and so did the sheep in a cattle truck. Directors like to direct – to show that they are in charge. That is their stock in trade. It is difficult enough to persuade human beings to behave as you wish them to. But sheep? Forget it. We brought them into the television centre for what, in normal circumstances, would have been a rehearsal. Why we bothered I shall never know. It was a scene of disorganised anarchy and another important issue, which I had forgotten, was that these gentle creatures – and especially when they are nervous and unsure – want to go to the lavatory. Or, more accurately – they relieve themselves wherever they wish. Finally we drove them back into their lorry to await the audience and the broadcast. But, as you can imagine, there was a lot of cleaning up to do. And my colleagues, the scene hands, firmly put their feet down – though they were cautious where they did it. They were adamant. There was nothing in their contracts which obliged them to tidy up sheep manure – although they used another word for it. So, in all the dignity of what I then perceived to be my high office, I found myself on my hands and knees in my John Michael suit bought at huge expense and with much vanity on the King's Road in Chelsea, sweeping up dung along the corridors, in reception and in the studio for more than an hour. Oh yes, and the show? I have wiped it from my memory bank. But it was surely chaos. And there was a lot of laughter – in my case it was hysterical. Since it was supposed to be an entertainment programme, I guess that mirth was what was required. But it was not my finest hour.

On another occasion a Somerset farmer came to the studios for a live broadcast about some riveting subject like land drainage. He was ruddy of face and bulging of biceps. I doubt that he had ever been further afield than Yeovil in his life. He had certainly never before been anywhere near television with all its daunting apparatus. He was nervous and understandably so. His seat was beside our veteran presenter. We went on the air and, almost immediately, the farmer, in his anxiety, started drumming on the table with his fingers. In those far off days we used lipstick microphones, which sat on the desks in small tripods. Nowadays everyone would have a personal system attached to a tie or a lapel. Through the mics the tapping fingers sounded like the charge of the Light Brigade in Tony Richardson's film. Something had to be done. All I could think of from the director's gallery was to ask the floor manager, through his earphones, to indicate to the presenter that he should take hold of the offending hand. In the middle of our transmission and while another guest was talking, he gently took hold of the farmer's hand and held it under the table. And I could see in that moment on that burly, sun-tanned face all his worst fears about film people confirmed. I will swear that he was thinking – they are not just like that; they actually do it on the air. At the end of the broadcast I hurried down to the studio floor to explain the situation to our guest. But he had already made a dash for it and was, even then, heading back home to his beautiful county. I will have a bet that he was never again tempted beyond its fertile borders. I dread to think what reports he took back with him about television and its strange people.

Every Tuesday morning at nine o'clock I leave home after completing my early morning duties and bicycle to school. I enjoy doing what I can to be helpful at our nearby Church of England junior school with its three hundred and sixty pupils aged from six to eleven years old. Bicycling is a pleasure. My first bike was a rusty wreck, which I rode as a six and seven year old round our family farm in Suffolk during the war. It had no rubber tyres. Rubber was a precious military commodity in those days. So I had to make do on my metal rims. Today I have a venerable machine from the 1950s. I bought it for twelve pounds in 1965 and sometimes rode it to work the thirteen miles to and from the Southampton studios. Milly is not allowed to come to school – and quite right too. So she sees me off with a quiet woof and gives me a flatteringly ecstatic welcome on my return. I wear no helmet or lycra gear. I have no wish to look more ridiculous than nature has made me or to attempt to mirror Spider Man. I do wear bicycle clips to prevent my corduroy trouser cuffs getting stained with oil or caught and torn in the chain. Sometimes, to the delight of the children, I forget to take them off before going into the classroom. It would be an insult to him but I like to think of myself as the Mr Chips of the place.

The New Forest today is teeming with bicyclists – serried ranks of grim, sour-faced blokes riding like Jehu and three-abreast along our narrow lanes. Many foresters dislike them and not just for their arrogance and bad manners. Signposts are turned so that the charging pack is directed up onto the traffic mayhem of the Salisbury highway. Hay and straw are placed strategically so that the commoners' animals fill the roads as they gather to eat, forcing the cyclists to slow down and to dismount as they pick their way between the piles of dung. If you are driving a car and slow down or give way to the bicycle pack, you seldom receive even a nod of acknowledgment. With horse-riders you always get a courteous 'thank you'. The two-wheeled tossers clearly believe that they are the kings of the road. Somebody should teach them some manners – a lost cause, I am afraid.

Milly likes bicycles in one sense at least. She is sorely tempted to chase after them barking and to bite their tyres or the feet of the riders. She too is being taught good behaviour. Not long ago we were out for a picnic near the village of Fritham with a bunch of friends. There must have been a dozen dogs of every shape and size. Milly was in her element, bossing everyone about and trying to organise people and their pets. Suddenly dreaded bicyclists hove into view, streaking along the skyline. There was an instant pause and then the whole pack set off in noisy pursuit, led by you know who. I knew that it would be hopeless but I waited a moment and then gave my firmest whistle and shout. Milly hesitated and, by some miracle, turned and led them all back to us. I would not have been more proud if I had been walking out to open the batting for England at Lords. I told Milly how very pleased I was with her, and I know that she understood. She lets me know that she understands compliments but cannot make head or tail of my insults.

It was in the late spring and before Milly came on the scene when Elisabeth and I set out for the West Country – but not on bicycles – to try to learn how to become sheep shearers. Before then we had paid the professionals to come to our patch to do this most complex and back-breaking job for us. Be under no illusions – the world record for taking the fleece off a struggling ewe is probably around the minute mark. The young Australians and New Zealanders and sometimes the Brits who came to Drove Cottage to help us out averaged, I would guess, between three and five minutes. Elisabeth and I, working together, take half an hour for each animal. So we are amateurs, and it is lucky for us that we do not have a thousand or more sheep to shear. We would have time for almost nothing else. The one thing which I might say in our favour is that I reckon that we cut the animals less than the speed merchants do. When the creature belongs to you, it is natural that you will take greater care not to wound it or to shed its blood.

We shear our small flock soon after lambing. So, when it is beginning to be warm in early June, we look at our diaries and find a suitable couple of days which we can put aside exclusively for the work. There is no point in doing this job in dribs and drabs. Milly had just arrived when we took the plunge and decided that, this year, we would take the fleeces off without skilled help. We were nervous. Would our training see us through? Would we have the strength to complete the task? Because Milly was new to us and to sheep, it was decided that she would be excluded. She had no say in the matter. If she had, she would have been outraged. But she was put in the house with the door firmly shut. Now there is one golden rule for Milly in her life at Drove Cottage. It has been promulgated and is enforced by my wife. Milly can wander where she will downstairs. But she is strictly forbidden to mount our staircase, which is more like the steep steps inside a double-decker bus. Even in the event of fire, flood, famine or pestilence Milly has to be a downstairs dog. So we get under way with the tricky job of shearing in a hurdle enclosure beyond the beech hedge in a small meadow thirty yards to the south-east of our house. We are old enough to know that,

Matilda gets her annual haircut

when you start a new work-skill, it pays to proceed slowly. The shearing clippers are sharp and fierce. I am guiding them with great caution along the backbone of the first ewe. The fleece is beginning to come away like magic. My concentration is absolute. Things are going well. Suddenly I hear my wife utter the nearest thing she knows to a foul oath and say, 'I just do not believe it.' I turn off the machine, nearly cutting myself in the process, and look around to see what emergency has happened. And there, yellow eyes blazing, is Milly standing upstairs in our bedroom window, paws on the sill and hind legs on our bed. She has realised that something important is going on. She has worked out how she can discover what it is. She has mounted the stairs for the first time in her life to find her grandstand view. She gets no marks for obedience. She gets a high score from me, though not from Elisabeth, for intelligence and intuition.

WHEN my first grandsons, George and Jack, were born, I was in my early fifties. Because of age vanity I did not wish to be called grandpa. Their parents decided to tell them to call me by my initials which are AJ. Soon after his fifth birthday, George and his family arrived in the New Forest from Bedfordshire, where they then lived. 'Hello, Age,' said George as he climbed out of the car, giving me a hug and my well-earned come-uppance. And so it has been ever since. Jack is now eighteen and George is twenty and they both still call me 'Age'. I dote on them both and am absurdly and boringly proud of them. In his 'A' level exams George won two A-stars and two As. Naturally, he told me nothing of this for three months until I forced it out of him. I often tell him that he is a 'one'. And so is his brother.

Their parents had a collie called Bob, the first of the breed that I had met. It is conceited of me to say so, but Bob came to adore me – and I him. He is the reason that my wife was eventually generous enough to buy Milly for me. One day he invited himself to lie on the sheepskin rug beside my bed while I was having an afternoon nap. There was outrage in certain quarters but this habit of his soon became a fixture. And he used to trot behind me all day back and forward as I drove the tractor across our meadows towing the roller or the chain harrow.

George and Jack Judd with their grandparents

I wept salt tears as we buried him in a place of honour in our fallen tree field when he died of cancer at the age of ten. I did not know it then but Bob made sure that, if ever I was to have a dog in the years ahead, it would be a collie. Rudyard Kipling, as so often, got it right:

> 'When the body that lived at your single will,
> With its whimper of welcome, is stilled (how still);
> When the spirit that answered your every mood
> Is gone – wherever it goes – for good,
> You will then discover how much you care
> And will give your heart to a dog to tear.'

Bob

Milly, like Bob patiently following the tractor, thinks that she would have made a good companion to a gallant knight in mediaeval times following her master close behind his stirrup. Some say that this was the role played by that handsome but now extinct dog, the Talbot, which still exists in heraldry today. Knights, alas, are not what they once were. They should be young and muscular and twenty years old, mounted on a mettlesome steed and armed with sword, lance and shield and protected by breastplate and full armour. Is there any more absurd spectacle than a late middle-aged man with reading glasses and a hernia calling himself a knight? In history these warriors were supposed to be pure and perfect and honourable. Nowadays, they are more often financiers who cheat their customers and lift their faces out of the trough with food all over their chins and gravy staining their striped shirt-fronts. These are contemptible figures of ridicule and fun – the nation's laughing-stock. Milly, I feel sure, would not want to be a companion to anyone like that, even if she has to put up with the eccentricities of her present master. In truth she is not very war-like at all, even if she does put on a show of defending her boss and his territory. She is terrified of the crack of my 12-bore or the snap of the .22 rifle or the squirrel-directed airgun. She is not keen on the sound of distant pigeon-scarers and waits anxiously for the inevitable and carefully-timed second bang. She keeps her distance when I am using the chainsaw on a fallen tree in our two-acre wood. And she even reacts badly when I am ringing the church bells at nearby Minstead on a Sunday morning. For this I cannot reproach her. Although it is not possible even for me to play a wrong note on a bell, it is certainly well within my capabilities to make an ugly noise. And I am the only, self-appointed member of the Minstead C team. When bell ringing goes badly it is not a pretty sound for man or beast. There is always a lot of shooting round our patch so poor Milly spends a fair amount of time running for cover. Her favourite air raid shelter is the cubby-hole below my desk. She seems to be at peace there and is comfortingly warm against my legs as I sit and write with my trusty fountain pen and my bottle of dark-blue ink. The barrage during the pheasant shooting season from October into February is particularly fierce and fearsome. And then there is the culling of the deer and all the controversy which that arouses. Beautiful and delicate creatures

Grandson George and friend

they are. But there are far too many of them for the Forest to sustain, so many would starve if they were not shot. The same is true of badgers. Our meadows, by the end of the winter months, often resemble the battlefields of Agincourt or Crécy after the true knights had finished trampling over them. The grass for the grazing animals is ruined. So what to do? I understand that not far short of two thousand deer were shot in the New Forest alone last year and that that number might be half of what is required. Of course, in this part of the country, you are sent to prison and fined if you shoot a badger. Alternatively, I have heard tell of peanut butter sandwiches with forty paracetamol included or of potatoes boiled in diesel (though not ideally on the kitchen stove) shoved down the mouth of the setts. Again, this would be breaking the law. But the problem still has to be solved. It is the same challenge as that of too many people having too many children in too small a world. And, magnificent animals though they may be, badgers are not the woolly cuddly toys that so many townsfolk take them to be. They are as tough as teak and red in tooth and claw, as our lovely hens will be glad to testify.

It sounds immoral I know, but sometimes I have a bath in Milly's bedroom. In a posh house I believe that it would be called the utility room. At Drove Cottage it is a fine jumble of clothes waiting to be washed, my shaving kit, the medicine cupboard, Milly's small mattress, sacks of dog food, umbrellas, trays, a pulley-maid with sheets hanging up to dry, the laundry cupboard and a selection of sponges, flannels, nail brushes and pumice stones. Once I am in the bath, Milly comes and puts her chin on the edge of the tub and looks anxiously at me as I wallow and splash. She is not sure what to make of a wet and naked master and has the feeling that something terrible is happening to me. She is definitely not a water dog and particularly if the water is warm and full of bubbles. She is more like the farm men of my youth, who used to sew up in October and not unsew again until March. The smell of a dirty dog is her idea of perfume. And, with some of the products on the market today, I think that she has a point. I have met collies which love water. They have never been in the springer spaniel or Labrador class, but then neither of those breeds is much good with sheep.

In the summer of 1986 I had the great good fortune to be invited to go to

Fremantle near Perth in Western Australia to direct a documentary about that year's 12-metre yacht race for the America's Cup. I know little about sailing, although, in 2013, I had the luck to be a junior member of the crew of Sky Hunter when she won the Round the Isle of Wight race against over 1600 other competitors in early June of that year. The British entry for the America's Cup was called White Crusader. The skipper was the talented and masterful Harold Cudmore. We were with him and his crew for five weeks to make our film, which was shown on the ITV network. It was called *Down for the Cup*. We had one day off during the shoot, although one of the chief joys of filming is that most location days feel like holidays. It was a Sunday, I remember, and I decided to have a day to myself, to walk along the beach, to swim when I was hot and to grab a fine fish lunch at a seaside restaurant or café before turning for home. The weather was perfect and I had covered four or five easy miles when I came upon a beach fisherman with his collie dog, which was rushing in and out of the foam and, every now and again, being bowled over by some of the stronger waves. It was a charming and amusing sight, so I sat on the beach and watched. After a while I walked over to the man, patted the dog, looked at his catch and asked him if there was a place where I could eat somewhere along the coast. He nodded. 'And how far is it from here?' I asked. 'I should say about four hundred and fifty miles,' he replied. That is Australia for you – a continent in its own right.

One secret Milly needs to learn is how to make friends with dogs and with people and how not to make enemies. It is a lesson that I also need to be taught. I have made plenty of foes in my long life. Some of them I am sad about – some I could not care less about. My best ever boss in my television years was called Greg Dyke. He was the man who set me on the road to becoming an independent film maker. He is, I suppose, fifteen years younger than I am, and I wondered at the time whether it would be difficult to be under the control of someone so much my junior. Because of his lack of superiority, his even character and his man management skills, he made it easy. Later he was to become Director General of the BBC – I would argue the most accomplished which that stuffy, over-managed organisation has ever had. He was torpedoed from his job by the deceit, treachery and chicanery of the Blair government. DGs at the BBC are almost invariably offered knighthoods. I have no idea whether or not Greg was. But I believe that I know the man well enough to promise that, had he been, he would have treated the invitation with the contempt and disdain which it deserves. Who on this earth would wish to be bracketed with that bunch of crooks, conmen and sycophants? Greg is now chairman of the Football Association and I hope that he may soon be having some fun sorting out the FIFA rogues. Decent man though he was, Michael Foot was not a great leader of the Labour Party. But at least, unlike Kinnock and many another one besides, he had the dignity to stick to his principles and to turn down the peerage, which could surely have been his. I am proud to be able to call Greg Dyke a friend. One of his repeated convictions was that a man is not worth much in life if he has made no enemies. It was a belief that he applied with some determination in his career and certainly in his relations with the high and the mighty. In a very different way my parents, with their deep and dogged religious attitudes, made enemies of those who disagreed with them or who attacked their faith. Yet I remember during the 1939-1945 war, when Germans were our bitter and brutal adversaries, how they often preached forgiveness and understanding. On our Suffolk farm during those savage years, prisoners of war from the local camp came to work in the fields and with the animals. As children these were, to us, like any other visitors to Hill Farm. We made friends with them, laughed and joked and played games around the straw stacks. It must have been strange for them to be involved in normal, family life in such unconventional circumstances. As Christmas approached my father had an idea. He went to see the commander of the PoW camp, a grizzled major of modest talents. Might the men, who had been coming every week to work with us, be allowed to travel to spend Christmas Day and to eat Christmas lunch at our home? We were all excited at the prospect. There was a long delay and much toing and froing in the corridors of the Ministry of Defence – in those far gone days, the War Office. It was rather as though we had suggested the opening up of a third front on the Chinese border. At last the word came through. It would be OK. And so, on 25th December, the three men came. We had managed to contrive simple gifts for them. There were some candles and modest decorations. We had a decent meal – probably boiled chicken or rabbit and apple pie. With wartime rationing there was certainly no turkey and plum pudding. There was no drink. Our home was an alcohol-free zone. But there was happiness and laughter – and tears. These Germans were simple men from the called-up ranks of the infantry. They had not seen their families for years. It was an act of love by my parents to have included them in our Christmas celebration, and it meant everything to the prisoners. It made the day for all of us too – an event which I have never forgotten. It taught me a great deal about friends – and enemies.

I once found myself making an enemy of a man from the Netherlands in Kenya. I was directing a musical film for the great Dutch firm Philips of Eindhoven. It was a movie of an African, catholic mass called the *Missa Luba*. Its memorable music was used to great effect by Lindsay Anderson in his gripping film *If …* about the joys, sorrows and madness of life in an English public school. We went on location around the wilds of East Africa and were looked after in tented luxury – conditions which put me in mind of Meryl Streep and Robert Redford in *Out of Africa*. It was a rare piece of good fortune to be involved in the project. Our shower was a bucket suspended in a tree with a rope tied to the handle so that you could tip water onto your head and body. The river water often had to be carried hundreds of yards to the camp. Our simple and excellent meals were eaten under the stars on trestle tables with white linen cloths and served by courteous Kikuyu men clad in pristine jackets. We were, amazingly, offered a choice of wine or beer with our food. To me this was extraordinary. But not, apparently, to the Dutch. One night a burly sound recordist called over the head waiter, showed him the bottle of Chardonnay and complained, 'This wine is not chilled.' I was speechless with anger at the man's insensitivity and ingratitude. The nearest power point was probably two hundred miles away.

I wanted to achieve a sequence in the film with three Masai warriors striding up over the skyline with their spears and silhouetted against the giant, red, rising sun of Africa. It meant an early call – 4.00 am if my memory is correct. Make no mistake. We were out in the wilds. In the night I was regularly awakened by big beasts purring gently as they brushed against the guy ropes of my tent. I did not much care to speculate what they might be. As we set out I asked the camp master whether my money and passport would be safe while we were away. We had a two mile march to our chosen location. The man looked at me as if I was mad. What could possibly go wrong out here in the bush? We only had wild animals for neighbours. Everything went well with the shoot and we returned at nine o'clock with the pictures and sounds which I was hoping to achieve. It had been a breathtakingly beautiful dawn. As soon as we arrived back at base I knew that something was wrong. My bag and the clothes in my tent had been gone through and disturbed. All my money – dollars and sterling – had vanished as well as my passport and other valuables. I reported this to the man in charge. He was naturally mortified. We got on with the rest of our day's work and that night, during supper, there was a great clamour from the lines where the men who were looking after us stayed. We jumped up and rushed over to the blazing campfire where they had been eating their meal. They had decided among themselves to conduct a strip search to make sure that none of them was the thief. They felt, with some justice, that their honour as a working unit was at stake. Alas, in the underpants of one of their number – a recently enlisted member of the team – they found my belongings. This wretched soul had been forced to stand on an upturned box with a noose around his neck. It is my honest belief that his colleagues intended to lynch him. We intervened. He was taken away by the bosses, tied up and, against my protests, locked for the night in the cab of one of the trucks. They insisted that it was for his own safety. And who can say that they were wrong? The next day he was driven to the road to Nairobi and left on the verge to make his own way home. It was several hundred miles away. It is fair to say that, for complex reasons, this sad and ugly incident coloured my attitude to travel, however exotic, from that day to this. Nowadays, with one or two exceptions, I prefer to stay at Drove Cottage.

I am an admirer of Noel Coward and his work. I took my beloved wife, Elisabeth, to one of his less distinguished musicals soon before we were married. The year must have been 1961. It was at the Savoy Theatre. The show is called *Sail Away*. Elaine Stritch was the magnificent star in the production which we saw. She sings: '*Why do the wrong people travel, travel, travel when the right people stay back home? What compels that mass mania to leave Pennsylvania and clack around like flocks of geese,*

Winter at Drove Cottage

demanding Dry Martinis on the Isles of Greece?' And so it proceeds in particularly Coward fashion. We have friends living in a sixteenth century paradise of a house in the Scottish borders and overlooking the beauty of those hills and out towards the Irish Sea. As a surprise the husband booked them on a Caribbean cruise. They drove down to Southampton. In the hangar there they assembled with the other two thousand passengers. The wife took one look at the throng and said, 'I am not going to spend four weeks with these people.' They drove back to Scotland. It was an expensive mistake and, no doubt, a snobbish attitude. But the point is well made. We human beings are not in the main, an attractive proposition – certainly not en masse. Compared to other living creatures we are rather ugly as well. And we do all seem to have the urge to travel to excess, no matter what the discomfort or the damage to the environment.

One last, brief tale out of Africa. I was directing a film in the Gambia in the 1970s. It was called *The Golden River*. There was much smuggling across the border into neighbouring Senegal. We managed to borrow, at great expense, a helicopter from the local air force there. My script demanded a long, aerial tracking shot from the river and over and across the capital, Banjul. It was not a difficult thing to achieve. But I do not suppose that this small, West African nation had ever seen such a machine as a chopper in those distant days. We swept in low over the outskirts sending flocks of egrets screaming into the sky. The air was calm. Our passage was as smooth as silk. At the end of the take the cameraman looked up at me smiling from his vantage point and said, 'Well, you won't be able to use a foot of that.' I thought that he was pulling my leg. But he was right. On almost every roof top were women lying stark naked and enjoying the warmth of the late afternoon sun. It was their custom in the Gambia. Milly would have been shocked. And I had to find another way of illustrating the words in my screenplay.

My wife, Elisabeth, is a marathon runner – several times in London, in the south where we live, in New York and Amsterdam. She is a glutton for this punishing kind of fun – even in her seventieth year. Milly also thinks that she would enjoy long distances. But even though she has unbounded energy, I doubt that she could keep going at her pace for more than twenty-six miles. And I am certain that she could not discipline herself to run more slowly. In America, about half way into the race, Elisabeth measured her length on the harsh, metal struts of the Queensborough Bridge and smashed her nose and face. The officials wanted to ambulance her straight to hospital, but she insisted that she had travelled all this way to run the marathon and that she was determined to complete the distance. They patched her up as best they could and she trotted the last twelve miles and crossed the finishing line looking like elephant woman. In Amsterdam I sat in the Olympic stadium on a bright morning watching as half a dozen men from Kenya and Ethiopia, loping like gazelles, led the pack out into the flatlands. Elisabeth was one of the fifteen thousand following in their wake. In what seemed like minutes later – it was probably closer to two hours – the six were back with us to complete their final lap round the stadium. As they approached, the phone in my pocket gave its irritation buzz. It was the Dutch friend with whom we had been staying in Wassenaar, 'Anthony,' he shouted. 'I am watching the marathon on television. Six African men have just run into the stadium. Where the hell is Elisabeth?'

Short of fire, famine and pestilence my wife runs every day of the year. She even goes out before breakfast when we are skiing. Sometimes she covers two miles. More often it is four, and regularly six. And, as the big day of a race approaches, it mounts to fifteen or more. In training she never runs over twenty miles. The theory is that the last six are so bloody that, if you run them before the marathon, you would probably decide to abandon the project altogether. If Milly is lucky and has been behaving well, she sometimes gets invited to go out on these early exercises. It is a treat for her because it is a different route from my morning rounds and much swifter and more adventurous. To polish her already shining halo, Elisabeth also picks up litter on these training runs, and Milly is pleased to try to help if she can. Over the years she will have picked up tens of tons of debris chucked out of car windows, discarded from bicycles or by ramblers and left behind by picnickers. Once she found a brace of pheasants, which we plucked and gutted and ate with pleasure. Usually the offerings are a great deal less attractive. And sometimes my wife staggers home, looking like Mother Christmas, with a bulging and heavy sack on her back. What is wonderful to relate is that the lanes around our village of Newbridge, unlike so much of the New Forest, are spectacularly clean and tidy and free of the usual filth of our selfish and careless twenty-first century. I often try to imagine what it is that allows people to chuck garbage down in our roads and streets. I am completely baffled by it. I always hoped that ours was a country peopled by civilised citizens.

One of the many treats we have to enjoy is our summer visit to the island of Tiree in the Inner Hebrides off the west coast of Scotland. If ever you listen to the early morning shipping forecast on BBC radio 4 at 5.20 in the morning, you will hear mention of 'Tiree automatic'. It is, put quite simply, paradise on earth. The agony for me of the six day break is having to leave Milly behind. The journey is too much for her. She does not like cars. We leave our cottage at 6.30pm and drop Milly off with our daughter, whose aristocratic Saluki, Prince, is willing to put up with the presence of a dog from the lower classes for a short while. We then drive through the night to the fine fishing port of Oban half-way up Scotland's western coastline. The magnificently old-fashioned Caledonian McBrayne ferry leaves from here at 7.00am. We take two-hour shifts with the driving and travel on wondrously empty motorways which, during the day, would be the kingdom of hell. A couple of driving sessions each and we are north-west of Glasgow at Crianlarich. After that it is a doddle. The solid, old ship steams westward with Mull to port and Ardnamurchan to starboard. After an hour we come to Tobermory and then out into the Irish Sea. On a fine day Skye is just visible to the north. On deck my heart is torn by the sight of a friendly border collie, which reminds me painfully of my Milly back down in Hampshire. This one is sporting a red spotted neckerchief and I vow that, when we get home, I shall tear in half one of my treasured handkerchiefs and tie one triangle around Milly's neck and one round Pedro, Elisabeth's favourite lamb. Soon we dock at Coll and a dozen cars and bicycles leave us for their destinations on that wild and beautiful island. And then, after nearly four hours at sea, our treasured Tiree heaves into view. As we pass the eastern end of the island we can see clearly from the ferry the small, white, hilltop house where we stay. Outside it and just visible, friends and family are waving sheets and blankets in welcome. It is tear-jerking stuff. And we know, at last,

Milly is more interested in listening to the Test Match than her master

that we are there. Tiree is empty, surrounded by white sand beaches peopled by sand-pipers, curlew, oyster catchers, pink-footed geese and dunlin. It boasts vast basking sharks and seals and kite-surfing, pottery and painting to bleed for, lobsters and whiskey, wild flowers and cowrie shells, walks and laughter and pints of beer and the very best of good company. And all-too-soon it is over and gone for another precious year. And we have the long journey south and the joy of a squirming Milly lying on her back and tying herself in knots to make us welcome. And finally the pride and pleasure in cutting in half my best red-spotted handkerchief and putting it carefully round her dear neck. When we are alone together she tells me that she thinks that it suits her quite well. I do not willingly criticise her but I fear that she may be just a little bit vain.